Rhoda Lederer, in company with her famous husband, Tony Lederer, was for many years one of the leading bridge teachers in the country. She holds the English Bridge Union's Honorary Teaching Diploma, and was for fifteen years Executive Secretary of the E.B.U.'s Teachers Association. She has now partially retired, though she keeps up with modern developments and the production of her ever-popular books which students find so readable, as well as the *Bridge Player's Acol Diary*. Her co-author, Dr David Griffiths, is also an experienced teacher, holding the E.B.U.'s Gold Level Diploma.

Their *Winning Ways at Bridge* proved a huge success, and now comes their latest collaboration, *Fits & Misfits*. This is a much neglected subject, and the authors hope that the book will help you to steer clear of those awful moments when dummy goes down and you see that you have landed in an impossible 5-1 fit when the 4-4 fit – had you discovered it – would have made the contract stone cold.

Other books on bridge:

ABC OF CONTRACT BRIDGE by Ben Cohen & Rhoda Lederer
ACOLITE's QUIZ by Rhoda Lederer
ALL ABOUT ACOL by Ben Cohen and Rhoda Lederer
BASIC ACOL by Ben Cohen and Rhoda Lederer
BEST BRIDGE HANDS by Rixi Markus
BID BOLDLY, PLAY SAFE by Rixi Markus
INSTRUCTIONS FOR THE DEFENCE by Jeremy Flint & David
    Greenwood
LEARN BRIDGE WITH THE LEDERERS by Tony & Rhoda
    Lederer
WHY YOU LOSE AT BRIDGE by S. J. Simon
WINNING WAYS AT BRIDGE by Rhoda Lederer & David Griffiths
YOUR LEAD PARTNER by Ben Cohen & Rhoda Lederer

FITS AND MISFITS

Rhoda Lederer

&

David Griffiths

UNWIN
PAPERBACKS

LONDON SYDNEY WELLINGTON

First published in Great Britain by Unwin ® Paperbacks,
an imprint of Unwin Hyman Limited, in 1989.

Unwin Hyman Limited
15–17 Broadwick Street
London W1V 1FP

Allen & Unwin Australia Pty Ltd
8 Napier Street, North Sydney, NSW 2060, Australia

Allen & Unwin New Zealand Pty Ltd with the Port Nicholson
Press
Compusales Building, Ghuznee Street, Wellington, New Zealand

British Library Cataloguing in Publicaton Data
Lederer, Rhoda
Fits and misfits.
1. Contract bridge, – Manuals
I. Title   II. Griffiths, David
795.41'5
ISBN 0–04–440452–2

Phototypeset by Input Typesetting Ltd, London
Printed in Great Britain by Cox & Wyman Limited, Reading.

Contents

Contents

Foreword

There is an old bridge adage which says 'Let the opponents play the misfits – we'll play the fits,' and this book is concerned with the achievement of that ideal.

It is a book about bridge, not any particular system, though obviously, coming from me, the bidding is somewhat Acol-orientated. It covers fits and misfits in all their aspects: how to recognise them; when to stretch the bidding; when to hang back; the need to bid your values once only; how to find fits on one-, two- and three-suiters in contested and un-contested sequences; doubling and redoubling situations; how to counter the opponents' transfer bids and other artificial gadgets; warning signs of misfits; how to escape the real horrors; when and when not to rescue; how to get the most out of your opponents' misfits and, finally, defensive strategy against these difficult hands.

Wherever possible, we have chosen simplicity. There are no complex gimmicks, and the book concentrates on commonsense advice. Much of the text is concerned with what can be learned from hands that have been dealt (and caused problems) in competitions.

I don't actually know of any other book which concentrates on this difficult subject so it is, I think, unique. It is not for beginners and is, in fact, more advanced than our *Winning Ways at Bridge*. But it was time I got away from teaching purely student players, and produced something for those who know their way about a pack of cards, yet really want to improve. For such a project David Griffiths was the perfect co-author for me.

Foreword

Although some of his modern ideas startle me at times, I always come around to agreeing, and working on this book with David has been very good for me.

I believe I am right in saying that the classic *Right Through the Pack* by Darvas & Hart, now sadly out of print, was for many years renowned for being the only bridge book completely free of errors. If *Fits & Misfits* follows in its footsteps, I should tell you that this is almost entirely due to Mr Philip Scull for checking the typescript and searching out errors in the analysis of the hands. So our sincere thanks goes to him for all the work he did.

Rhoda Lederer
January 1989

Introduction

There are many ways of valuing a bridge hand. Everyone knows the Milton Work point count of 4 points for an ace, 3 for a king, 2 for a queen and 1 for a jack. These are the high card points (HCP) but most players add distributional points (DP) also, for example, 1 extra point for a five-card suit, 2 extra points for a six card suit, etc.

Another method is to count Quick Tricks, i.e. tricks that can be taken during the *first two* rounds of a suit (you must assume that the third round will be trumped). Thus an ace = 1 Quick Trick, K-Q is 1 Quick Trick, A-K is 2 Quick Tricks; A-Q is 1½ Quick Tricks and K-x is ½ Quick Trick. This scale is similar to defensive tricks or Honour Tricks, an early method of hand evaluation.

Finally, it is very useful to count Playing Tricks, i.e. tricks that you expect to make if the contract is played in your long suit. Here you have to make some assumptions about how the hand will play. Firstly, it is simplest to assume that your partner has two cards in your long suit. If he has more, you will be delighted, if he has a singleton or void you will be disappointed, but you must assume something. Then assume that all suits will break normally, so that you can gauge how many tricks you will make. With regard to the position of missing high cards, assume average luck, for example, that half your finesses will succeed; if two honours are missing in a suit, assume that they are split, one in each opponent's hand. Thus, a suit such as A-K-x-x-x-x would be counted as 5 Playing Tricks, assuming that partner has two cards of the suit and that the opponent's cards split 3-2 (the normal break). A suit such as A-Q-10 would be counted as 2 Playing Tricks, assuming that one finesse would be right.

Thus any bridge hand should be looked at with as many valuation yardsticks as possible to gain an accurate idea of its potential.

	Points HCP DP		Playing tricks	Quick tricks
♠ K Q J 10 3	6	1	4	1
♡ 3	–	–	–	–
♢ K Q J	6	–	2	1
♣ A 10 4 2	4	–	1	1
	17		7	3

The hand shown above has a total of 17 points, should take three defensive tricks and, if played in spades, should make seven playing tricks.

However, this is only the *initial valuation*. The actual worth of the hand changes as the bidding progresses so the valuation must be constantly updated. For example, if you open 1♠ and your partner responds in clubs this would solidify your hand beautifully and your thoughts would turn towards exploring for a slam. However, if your partner responds in hearts, it would be a misfitting feature, facing your singleton, and your ambitions would probably not go beyond game. Similarly, if your opponent overcalled with clubs and your partner was silent, you could see yourself with a possible three losers in clubs, in addition to three missing aces, and you would not be inclined to compete too hard even for the part-score.

Sensitivity to the degree of fit or misfit on a hand is the hallmark of a good bidder. Let's just look to see what happens when there is no fit:

(a) No fit . . . no finessing. For example, ♣ x-x-x in the West hand opposite ♣ K-J-9-x in East can produce 2 tricks with average luck (three if very lucky) but none at all if there is a club void in the West hand and the suit has to be led from East.

(b) No fit . . . no entries. For example, ♣ x opposite ♣ K-Q-J-10-x can produce no tricks at all if the East hand has no entries and the opponents know when to take their ace.

(c) No fit . . . no suit establishment. Thus ♣ x-x opposite ♣ A-K-Q-x-x-x is worth six tricks on normal breaks, but if there are no outside entries ♣ x opposite ♣ A-K-Q-x-x-x could produce only three tricks and void opposite ♣ A-K-Q-x-x-x will produce no tricks at all. In this extreme example, each low card in partner's suit that is removed from the West hand results in three fewer tricks.

Partnership hands that contain a total misfit in every suit are, fortunately, rare, but in this book we shall be concentrating on telling the difference between hands which fit well, and which should be bid up to the hilt, and those with misfitting features, which should be treated with a great deal of caution.

1 Fits Part 1

Partnership hands which have considerable strength and which fit well can often be played in a game or higher level contract. To make the most of them, however, one has to have a sound bidding structure and the apparatus to discover if there are any quick losers. Most players use a slam convention to find out how many aces and kings the partnership has and we don't propose to go into any details of these well-known methods here. What is often more important, however, is to know exactly *which* aces and kings your partner has, and this can be done quite simply by 'cue bidding'.

Once you have agreed a trump suit with your partner, cue bidding is a method of telling partner whether you can control the early rounds of play in side suits, either with a first round control (ace or void) or a second round control (king or singleton). Worry about losing the first two tricks in the side suit may be the only thing that is holding partner back from bidding a slam. In the simple style of cue bidding that we advocate, first round controls are bid before second round controls and the cheapest cue bid is always chosen. By doing this, there is the important negative inference that when you bypass a certain suit, then you do not have the appropriate control in that suit. For example:

North	South
1♠	3♠ (agrees trump suit)
4♦ (first round control of diamonds, but lacking first round control of clubs)	

If South's clubs are poor he will know that a slam is unlikely even if he has good diamonds and hearts, and the partnership will not progress beyond 4♠.

Of course, a player never cue bids the trump suit because that would be simply a sign off to a cue bidding sequence.

When a player has shown his first round controls and wishes to progress further, he can show his second round controls in one of three ways, either by rebidding the suit in which he has already shown first round control, or by bidding the suit in which his partner has shown first round control or by cue bidding a suit which he has bypassed to deny first round control. Some examples follow later.

On the way to a slam one of the players may have made a *jump shift*, for example 1♣ – 2♠, which is forcing to game. This, of course, shows a strong hand and the ability to control the subsequent auction. The jump shift can be made on strong hands that are either balanced or have good trump support or have a strong outside suit of their own. Which of these three hand types the jump shift was based on will be revealed on the next round. We don't recommend making a jump shift on strong two-suiters as there may not be sufficient bidding space left to describe the hand shape accurately.

When your partner has made a jump shift over your opening bid, it is best to make your planned rebid as you would have done over a simple response from him. Your rebid, of course, is one level higher than you had planned, but it is your partner who has raised the level, not you. Thus if you planned to open 1♦ and to bid 1NT over

1♠, you would now rebid 2NT over 2♠. Don't make the mistake of bidding 3NT now because you know your partner is strong. The sequence 1◇ – 2♠, 3NT shows a hand that would open 1◇ and rebid 2NT over 1♠, and you must not mislead your partner.

The play: In many suit contracts, the simple procedure of counting your losers, then counting your winners and making sure they add up to thirteen will pinpoint the crucial features of the hand and suggest an appropriate line of play.

On other hands you will have to work harder for ways of making extra tricks. One useful method is to obtain a 'ruff and discard' by forcing the opponents to lead a suit in which both you and dummy have none left, so that you can ruff in one hand and, at the same time, discard a loser from the other hand. Similarly, it will help you if the opponents can be made to lead a suit in which, for example, you hold Q-x-x and dummy holds J-x-x. If you play the suit yourself, you may take no tricks at all, but if the opponents lead it, you have only to play low in the second hand to be relatively sure of one trick. Both these methods will require you to put the opponent on lead at the right time when he has nothing but helpful cards left, i.e. to execute a throw-in.

For example:

♠ K J 9 3 2   ♠ A Q 10 8 4
♡ K 4 2   ♡ A 7 3
◇ A 10 3   ◇ K J 2
♣ K 5   ♣ A 7

Suppose that you are West and that North leads the ♡Q against your contract of 6♠ on the hands shown above. There are eleven tricks on top (five spades, two hearts, two clubs and two diamonds). A third trick might develop from diamonds but you don't want to guess who has the

$\diamondsuit$Q. So the way to play the hand is to win the lead, draw trumps, cash the ♣ A-K and the other top heart and exit with a low heart. If the opponents return a club or a heart you will discard a diamond from one hand and ruff in the other; if they return a diamond you need only play low second in hand to assure yourself of three diamond tricks.

Another method of developing an extra trick is by a squeeze. We don't intend to go into the details of this technique here (there are plenty of books that do), but just to point out that there are two sorts of menace (or threat) that you can bring to bear against an opponent (a) a two-card menace such as A-J in a suit when he has K-Q, so if he throws one away both your cards will make tricks and (b) a one-card menace such as your K against his A or your 9 against his 10 (assuming there are no higher cards of the suit left) or even your 2 against his 3. In one of the most simple types of squeeze, menaces in declarer's and dummy's hands are directed against one unfortunate opponent, who finds that he can't keep all his guards. The ingredients are a squeeze card (usually the last trump or the last card of a side suit) plus a one-card menace, plus an entry to the two-card menace in the hand opposite. Also it is quite possible that both menaces are in the same hand facing the squeeze card.

♠ 6	You are West, with both sides vulner-
$\heartsuit$ Q 9 8 7 5	able. You open 1$\heartsuit$ and your partner
$\diamondsuit$ K 10 7 5	responds 2♣. You rebid 2$\diamondsuit$ and he
♣ A K 2	bids 3$\heartsuit$. Do you go on ?

So the bidding has been:

	West	East
	1$\heartsuit$	2♣
	2$\diamondsuit$	3$\heartsuit$
	?	

Although it may not be obvious, West should try 4$\heartsuit$

now. It is not justified on the point count, but there is an excellent fit in two suits, which makes all the difference.

The full deal:

♠ 6		♠ J 5
♡ Q 9 8 7 5	N	♡ K J 2
◇ K 10 7 5	W E	◇ Q J 8
♣ A K 2	S	♣ Q 7 6 5 3

There are just the three aces to lose. The contract will make on normal breaks, so this is a sound game contract, made on only a combined 22 high card points because each player has high cards in his partner's suit.

♠ 9 5
♡ A K 7 5
◇ K J 9 8 4 2
♣ 8

You are East, with both sides vulnerable. You open 1◇ and your partner responds 1♡. What is your rebid?

With such a lovely fit for your partner's suit, and a six-card suit of your own, it is worth stretching to 3♡ on this hand. This will also have the effect of keeping your opponents out of the auction. Over your 3♡, your partner goes to 4♡.

The bidding:

West	East
	1◇
1♡	3♡
4♡	

North leads the ♠ *A-K and switches to the* ♡3 *against West's contract of* 4♡. *Move over to the other side of the table now and plan the play by West.*

♠ 4 2	N	♠ 9 5
♡ Q J 6 4 2	W E	♡ A K 7 5
◇ A 7	S	◇ K J 9 8 4 2
♣ J 7 3 2		♣ 8

Planning and play: Without the heart switch, West might have been able to ruff three clubs but he can no longer do this, as the opponents will lead another trump when they win the first club trick. West, therefore, must set up the diamonds but he must be careful to preserve an entry to the East hand.

West wins the heart switch with the ♡A and leads another heart to the ♡Q. He plays the ◇A, ◇K and ruffs a diamond with the ♡J. Now he can re-enter the East hand with the ♡K and run the established diamonds.

Postscript: The contract may fail if one opponent started with four trumps or with three trumps and only a singleton diamond, but it has very good chances of success. Again the hands are not strong in high card points but they fit well.

♠ K 5 2	You are West, with neither side
♡ A 9 6	vulnerable. Your partner deals and
◇ K J 7 3 2	bids 1♡. You respond 2◇ and he
♣ 6 4	now bids 3♠. What do you make of
	that?

If the bidding had simply been 1♡ - 2◇, 2♠ then partner's 2♠ rebid would have been an unconditionally forcing reverse. But he has rebid 3♠, an unnecessary jump, which is interpreted as an advance cue bid, agreeing your diamond suit and announcing first round control of spades. You can co-operate by bidding 4♡, showing first round control of the suit and, because you bypassed clubs, showing that you lack first round club control. Your partner next bids 5♣ to show his club control. You can now show your second round control of spades by bidding 5♠, the suit in which your partner has already shown first round control, and your partner, suitably encouraged, bids 7♢.

The bidding:

	West	East
		1♡
	2♢	3♠*
	4♡*	5♣*
	5♠*	7♢

* cue bids

North leads the ♠Q against West's contract of 7♢. Plan the play.

♠ K 5 2		♠ A 8
♡ A 9 6	N	♡ K Q 5 4 3
♢ K J 7 3 2	W E	♢ A Q 9 4
♣ 6 4	S	♣ A 3

Planning and play: Provided the hearts are no worse than 4-1, and the trumps no worse than 3-1 there should be no problem. Simply draw trumps, play off the top hearts and ruff out the ♡J. You will make two spades and a spade ruff, four hearts, five diamonds and the ♣A.

Postscript: It's the fit in both red suits that makes the contract good. One can even cope with a 4-1 heart break provided the diamonds don't split badly too, so the contract is a sound one.

♠ A J 8 6 2   You are West, with East-West
♡ K J 9 2   vulnerable. You open 1♠, North
♢ A Q   overcalls with 2♣ and your partner
♣ 8 7   bids 3♡. What is your rebid?

Over a response of 2♡ from partner you would have bid
3♡ so over 3♡ you must bid 4♡. Your partner now bids
4♣. What do you do now?

Your partner is not signing off. He is merely clarifying
the type of hand on which he made the jump shift, namely
a hand with a big trump fit. You have nothing to be
ashamed of and can make a try with a cue bid of 5♢,
showing first round control of diamonds but lacking first
round control of clubs (your opponent's suit). If partner
can't guard the clubs he would now sign off in 5♠, but
in practice he bids 6♠.

The bidding:

West	North	East	South
1♠	2♣	3♡*	NB
4♡	NB	4♠†	NB
5♢	NB	6♠	

*Jump shift   † not a sign-off

*North leads the ♣K against West's contract of 6♠. Plan
the play.*

♠ A J 8 6 2   ♠ K Q 4 3
♡ K J 9 2   ♡ A Q 6 5 4
♢ A Q   ♢ 10 6
♣ 8 7   ♣ A J

Planning and play: There are twelve tricks on top but
you might as well look for a thirteenth if you can do so
with no extra risk. It looks as if North has led from the
♣ K-Q, and if he has the ♢K as well you may be able
to squeeze him.

Play the ♣A. Run all the spades followed by all the hearts. Look for signs of discomfort from North. If he throws his ♣Q, your ♣J will make. If he parts, grudgingly, with diamonds your ◇A may fell his ◇K.

The end position:

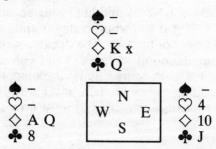

The ♣J is a one-card menace, and the ◇ A-Q is the two-card menace. On the last heart (the squeeze card) West can throw a club but North is helpless.

♠ A 2
♡ A Q 10 6 4
◇ J 7
♣ K J 9 7

You are West, dealer with North-South vulnerable. You open 1♡ and your partner responds 3♣. You raise to 4♣ and he bids 4♡. Do you go on?

Yes, why not? You have fifteen high card points and your partner has forced and then agreed your suit, so the world is your oyster. Show him your first round control of spades by bidding 4♠. Over 4♠ he bids 5♣. So the bidding has been:

West	East
1♡	3♣ (jump shift, forcing)
4♣	4♡ (agrees suit)
4♠ (cue bid)	5♣ (cue bid)
?	

Do you co-operate now by bidding your second round control of clubs? Not if you want to stay friends with your partner. A six level contract may be decidedly too much, considering your diamond weakness, and you must sign off in 5♡. He may, of course, have a diamond control and carry on bidding over your 5♡, but that is up to him. You have done all that you can and must now stop.

The full deal:

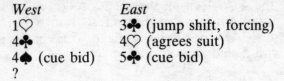

♠ A 2
♡ A Q 10 6 4
♢ J 7
♣ K J 9 7

♠ K J 5
♡ K J 9 8 7
♢ Q 9
♣ A Q 5

The opponents will take the first two diamond tricks, so the hand illustrates one of the main advantages of cue bidding in keeping you out of bad slams. There are very few disadvantages. Many cue bids are made at the four level (even at the three level in some cases) and there is often room, if you wish, to continue on to a 4NT Blackwood or other slam convention, and so to get the best of both worlds.

2   Fits   Part 2

This chapter continues the theme of hands that fit well in at least one suit. When strong, these can lead to slam contracts, provided the partnership possesses the necessary *controls* in the side suits. We shall again be dealing with cue bids, and introducing some further examples of situations in which the trump suit is agreed *by inference* before cue bidding begins.

It was explained in the last chapter that it is not possible to cue bid in the trump suit itself, because partner will think that you are simply signing off. However, if you have agreed a trump suit, are confident that there are no losers in the side suits and are thinking of a grand slam, it's possible to investigate partner's high card holding in the agreed trump suit by a convention known as the *Grand Slam Force*. Using this, a direct bid of 5NT (bypassing the ace enquiry of 4NT) is forcing and demands information about partner's holding in the trump suit itself. In the simplest version of this convention (the Culbertson Grand Slam Force), partner simply responds seven of the agreed trump suit if he possesses two of the top three honours in trumps, but signs off in six if he doesn't. (However, see p. 94–95 of *Bridge Conventions Made Clear* by Rhoda Lederer for some useful variations.)

In the play, declarer must do his best to keep communications open between his own hand and dummy, so the matter of entries is often of vital importance, as we shall see in some of the following deals. In addition, the way in which declarer handles individual suits is crucial to his success, so a few words of advice are given below. How declarer handles a suit will depend, amongst other things, on the cards he and dummy hold in the suit, on the number of entries in each hand, and on the content of the whole hand. For example, his decision on whether to finesse against the queen of trumps or play for the drop will depend, not only upon the odds, but also upon whether he can afford to risk losing the lead, and whether he has some other suit he must develop quickly.

It is, therefore, rather artificial to consider a single suit in isolation but there are a few preliminary points about suit handling that are worth making before starting to consider complete hands.

One question declarer must ask himself is how many tricks he wants from the suit and how many he can afford to lose. For example, if declarer (West) has ♢ x-x-x opposite ♢ A-Q-10-x-x and needs all five tricks, he will have to finesse the ♢ 10 and return to his hand to finesse the ♢Q, hoping that North has both ♢K and ♢J. If he wants to be fairly sure of four tricks in the suit without losing more than one it is best to finesse the ♢Q first and finesse the ♢10 later. Of course, if he needs just two tricks from the suit *without loss*, it is also right to finesse the ♢Q.

A common mistake with a holding such as ♣ J-5-3 opposite ♣ A-Q-10-6-2 is to lead the ♣J. The suit is nowhere near solid enough for that. An example follows below.

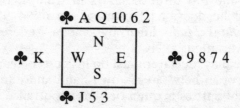

♣ A Q 10 6 2

♣ K | N W E S | ♣ 9 8 7 4

♣ J 5 3

If South leads the jack, a winner will be set up in the

East hand. The better play (assuming there are enough entries to repeat the manoeuvre if necessary) is to lead *low* towards the two honours. Also, declarer should avoid taking any finesse prematurely, so if he has to make three tricks from a suit such as ♡ x-x-x opposite ♡ A-K-J, he should cash the ♡A first, then return to his own hand to take the finesse. Who knows, the player who sits over the ♡ A-K-J may hold the singleton ♡Q, so declarer must give himself every chance.

The following hand illustrates the importance of suit handling technique. South plays in 3NT against the lead of the ♠5.

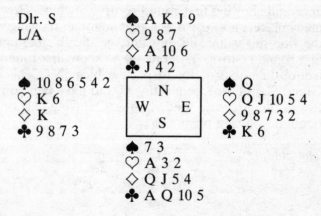

```
Dlr. S          ♠ A K J 9
L/A             ♡ 9 8 7
                ◇ A 10 6
                ♣ J 4 2
♠ 10 8 6 5 4 2       N        ♠ Q
♡ K 6          W       E      ♡ Q J 10 5 4
◇ K                S          ◇ 9 8 7 3 2
♣ 9 8 7 3                     ♣ K 6
                ♠ 7 3
                ♡ A 3 2
                ◇ Q J 5 4
                ♣ A Q 10 5
```

It would be a mistake to finesse the spades on the first round so South puts up dummy's ♠A, dropping the ♠Q and exposing the spade position. Now he leads a *low* club and if East plays low, finesses the ♣10. Now a *low* diamond towards the two honours in dummy, catching the ◇K. Now another low club picks up the ♣K and the marked finesse of the ♠9 ensures that declarer makes four spade tricks in addition to four clubs, four diamonds and the ♡A, thirteen tricks in all on a balanced 26 points. However, if he tries the ♠J at trick 1, the defenders will

13

force out his ♡A. Then, if he does not know how to handle the minor suits, he may even go down in 3NT.

  ♠ K 10 9 6 5 4 3 You are West, with neither side
  ♡ 5 3 vulnerable. What is your opening
  ♢ A 7 bid on this hand?
  ♣ 7 4

This weak one-suited hand is best opened with a pre-emptive bid of 3♠. North passes and your partner responds 4♣. Traditionally, this is a cue bid, showing slam interest, agreeing spades as the trump suit by inference and showing first round control of clubs. However, many players now use it as a general force, showing where the side-suit values lie, but not specifically guaranteeing first round control. You bid 4♢ to show first round control of diamonds and your partner bids 5NT. This is the Grand Slam Force, requesting you to bid 7♠ if you have two of the three top spade honours. Having only one top honour, you sign off in 6♠.

The bidding:

	West	East
	3♠	4♣
	4♢	5NT
	6♠	

North leads the ♣Q against West's contract of 6♠. Plan the play.

♠ K 10 9 6 5 4 3   ♠ A 8 2
♡ 5 3   N   ♡ A K Q J
♢ A 7   W   E ♢ 6 4 2
♣ 7 4   S   ♣ A 6 3

Planning: Despite your pre-emptive opening your partner, with six top tricks, was certainly justified in looking for a slam. All should be well if the spades split 2-1 but it would be sensible to cater for a possible 3-0 break. The lead has exposed your club loser so you will have to get rid of it quickly.

The play: Win with the ♣A. Cash ♠K and ♠A. If trumps split 3-0, leave the opponents' trump winner where it is and cash ♡ A-K-Q, discarding a club on the ♡Q. If both opponents have followed to the third heart, continue with the ♡J and discard your losing diamond.

Postscript: 6♠ will make even if the trumps are 3-0 provided that both opponents follow to the first two rounds of hearts; if they ruff the third round you still discard a club, and the ♠8 provides an entry to dummy's last heart. 7♠ will make if trumps are 2-1, so the Grand Slam is a reasonable prospect.

♠ K 9 3	You are West, with East-West
♡ J 10 8 6 5 2	vulnerable. Your partner opens 1♣
◇ Q 5 3	and, over your response of 1♡, he
♣ 5	rebids 3NT. What do you bid now?

You would be foolish to pass and hope that partner could bring in your heart suit, because your hand is so short of entries. You must play in your long suit, so you have to bid 4♡.

North leads the ♣2 against West's contract of 4♡. Plan the play.

♠ K 9 3		♠ A Q 4
♡ J 10 8 6 5 2	N	♡ A
◇ Q 5 3	W E	◇ A J 10 8
♣ 5	S	♣ A 9 7 4 3

Planning: Partner's hearts are disappointing. You would usually expect him to have a better fit for your suit before he leaps to game level. 3NT would have been difficult to manage and, although 4♡ does not look too bad, you will have to be careful not to lose a diamond trick and three hearts.

The play: Having won the first trick with the ♣A and cashed dummy's ♡A, you must return to your hand with the ♠K and continue with the hearts. You can't go wrong if hearts split 3-3 but, to save the loss of three heart tricks when hearts split 4-2, you must lead a low heart, not the ♡J, hoping to find one of the opponents with a doubleton honour. If either opponent holds ♡ K-Q-9-x or better you will always lose three trumps but the lead of a low heart to the second round of the suit pays off if one opponent has ♡ K-9-x-x or ♡ Q-9-x-x, for his partner will have a doubleton honour.

The full deal:

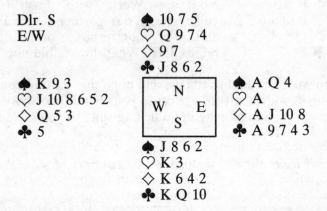

```
Dlr. S          ♠ 10 7 5
E/W             ♡ Q 9 7 4
                ◇ 9 7
                ♣ J 8 6 2
♠ K 9 3                          ♠ A Q 4
♡ J 10 8 6 5 2        N          ♡ A
◇ Q 5 3          W       E       ◇ A J 10 8
♣ 5                  S           ♣ A 9 7 4 3
                ♠ J 8 6 2
                ♡ K 3
                ◇ K 6 4 2
                ♣ K Q 10
```

Postscript: The mistaken lead of the ♡J or ♡10 to the second round of the suit would leave declarer with three heart losers, in addition to the ◇K.

♠ —
♡ K 10 9 8 6 5 4 3 2
◇ Q
♣ 7 6 4

You are West, with both sides vulnerable. Your partner, East, deals and opens 1◇. What do you respond?

You are certainly going to play this hand in hearts but it is just a question of how many to bid. You *could* start slowly with 1♡ but there doesn't seem to be much point in giving partner the opportunity to pass below game level. Even more important you may let the opponents into the bidding and they may reach a successful spade contract. If you bid 4♡ straight away, is there any chance that you will miss a slam? No, it is extremely unlikely that partner will have the necessary top cards in hearts, diamonds and clubs to prevent you from losing two tricks. You, therefore, bid 4♡, and this closes the auction.

North leads the ◇J against West's contract of 4♡. South wins with ◇A and switches to ♠4. Plan the play.

♠ —
♡ K 10 9 8 6 5 4 3 2
◇ Q
♣ 7 6 4

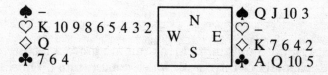

♠ Q J 10 3
♡ —
◇ K 7 6 4 2
♣ A Q 10 5

Planning: You have lost one diamond trick and will lose at least two hearts. You must ruff the spade return and set about drawing trumps. You have to decide how to handle the trump suit. If opponent's trumps are 4-0 you will always lose three trump tricks, if 2-2 you can only lose two. If the trumps split 3-1, how you play them will be critical. The missing cards are ♡A, ♡Q, ♡J and ♡7. If the ♡7 is a singleton you will lose three heart tricks whichever card you lead. If the ♡A is a singleton (one of the remaining chances) it will pay you to lead low but if either the ♡Q or ♡J is a singleton (two of the remaining chances) it will pay you to lead the ♡K, to hold your heart losers to two.

The play: Win the spade switch and lead the ♡K, continuing trumps when you can. When it comes to the play of the club suit you will have to risk the finesse of the ♣Q. You need just two club tricks and you can throw your third club on the ◇K.

The full deal:

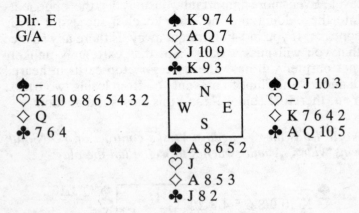

Dlr. E
G/A

♠ K 9 7 4
♡ A Q 7
◇ J 10 9
♣ K 9 3

♠ −
♡ K 10 9 8 6 5 4 3 2
◇ Q
♣ 7 6 4

♠ Q J 10 3
♡ −
◇ K 7 6 4 2
♣ A Q 10 5

♠ A 8 6 5 2
♡ J
◇ A 8 5 3
♣ J 8 2

Postscript: Voids in partner's suit are more a feature of later chapters of this book, which concentrate on misfits. A nine-card suit, however, requires practically no fit from partner, but still needs to be played with care.

♠ A K J 7 5 2
♡ A K 3
◇ 8
♣ Q 5 3

You are West, vulnerable against non-vulnerable opponents. You deal and open 1♠. Your partner responds 2♣. What is your rebid?

If partner had responded 2◇, your singleton, you would probably have been right to downgrade the hand and to consider carefully before rebidding 3♠. His club

response, however, greatly supports your own club holding and implies that the hands fit well, so you can confidently bid 3♠, or even a full-blooded 4♠. Although
partner (hand shown below) has only just scraped up his
2♣ response, his ♠ Q-6 gives excellent solidity to your
six-card suit, and even if you bid only 3♠, he will probably raise you to 4♠.

The bidding: West   East   West   East
                 1♠   2♣   or   1♠   2♣
                 4♠   3♠   4♠

*Against West's contract of 4♠, North leads the ♠ 10. Plan
the play.*

♠ A K J 7 5 2   ♠ Q 6
♡ A K 3   N   ♡ J 10 2
♢ 8   W   E   ♢ J 4
♣ Q 5 3   S   ♣ A 9 8 7 4 2

Planning: You could lose one heart trick, one diamond
and two clubs (if North has ♣K). You are short of entries
to dummy, so you may not be able to play the club suit
in the most efficient way.

The play: Draw trumps. Duck a round of clubs and,
when you regain the lead, duck a second round of clubs.
Unless the clubs break badly, your ♣A will drop the
opponent's remaining clubs and you can discard a heart
on a club winner.

Postscript: The probability of a 4-0 club split is less than
10%, so the contract has every chance of success.

♠ –
♡ A J 10 6 5 2   You are West. What is your opening
♢ K 9   bid on this hand?
♣ A K Q 7 5

The distribution makes this an extremely powerful hand. It is not strong enough for a 2♣ opener, but there should be little difficulty in wrapping up at least eight tricks so you open with 2 of the longer suit, 2♡. Your partner responds 3♡. What do you bid now?

The single raise of an Acol 2 opener is stronger than a double raise, guaranteeing trump support and some outside values. This solidifies your hand beautifully and you should now make a forward-going move with a cue bid of 3♠, your cheapest first round control. To this partner responds 4◇, showing first round control of diamonds, the best possible news you could have. It now appears that the only likely loser is in the trump suit itself. You can enquire about the quality of partner's trumps by using the Grand Slam Force. As explained on p. 11 the simplest form of this convention employs a direct bid of 5NT, requesting partner to bid 7 of the agreed trump suit if he has two of the three top honours, otherwise to sign off in six. As partner holds both king and queen of trumps (see below) he now bids 7♡.

The bidding:

West	East
2♡	3♡
4♣	4◇
5NT	7♡

North leads the ◇J against West's contract of 7♡. Plan the play.

```
       ♠ -                            ♠ 8 7 5 2
       ♡ A J 10 6 5 2      N          ♡ K Q 9
       ◇ K 9           W       E      ◇ A 7 2
       ♣ A K Q 7 5         S          ♣ 10 9 8
```

Planning and play: It looks very easy with a likely six heart tricks, two diamonds and five clubs. However, it would be wise to win the first trick with the ◇K and,

after drawing trumps, to test the clubs by playing
♣A-K. Then, if you discover that South has four clubs
to the jack, you will be able to enter dummy with the
♢A and run the ♣10 through him.

♠ A Q 10 2	You are West, dealer, with both sides
♡ A 10 8 6 5 4	vulnerable. You open 1♡ and rebid
♢ 8 6	2♡ over partner's response of 2♢.
♣ Q	Partner now bids 4♣. What do you
	bid?

Partner's second bid of 4♣ is an unnecessary jump, agreeing hearts as the trump suit and cue-bidding first round
control of clubs. This greatly improves your hand and
you should be pleased to co-operate in a forward-going
move by bidding 4♠ to show first round control of that
suit. Your partner now bids 6♡, which becomes the final
contract.

The bidding:

West	East
1♡	2♢
2♡	4♣
4♠	6♡

Although partner has 16 high card points (see below) he
did not force on the first round but waited until he knew
where the partnership was going before bidding strongly.
He may have overdone it a bit from there on, but at least
it should be interesting to play.

North leads the ♣2 against West's contract of 6♡. Plan the play.

```
♠ A Q 10 2              N          ♠ J 3
♡ A 10 8 6 5 4    W         E     ♡ K 9 3
♢ 8 6                   S          ♢ A K J 10 9
♣ Q                                ♣ A 9 4
```

Planning: You will have to win with the ♣A at trick one, as you can't afford to risk a club loser. Then if the hearts split 2-2 you will merely have to play on diamonds to be sure of 12 tricks. If the hearts are distributed in such a way that you lose one trick in the suit, then you have a choice of possible actions still available to you. The skill in playing the hand will be to make the most of your chances.

The play: Win with the ♣A. Play a heart to the ♡A and if both opponents follow, a heart back to the ♡K. If one of the opponents has a winning heart remaining, leave it where it is and cash ♢ A-K. If the ♢Q falls, simply continue diamonds and discard a spade; if one of the opponents ruffs, the ♡9 will provide an entry to dummy's remaining diamonds. If the ♢Q doesn't fall, lead the ♠J, intending to finesse and to lead a second spade from dummy if the finesse is successful. However, if South has the ♠K and covers, win with the ♠A, cash another top spade and ruff the ♠2 in dummy for your twelfth trick.

Postscript: The play looks easy. Simply cash ♡ A-K, then ♢ A-K and, if neither works, finesse the spade. Yet in a good standard duplicate event several declarers failed to make twelve tricks. North had the ♠K and South had the ♣K and the doubleton ♢ Q-x.

♠ K 10 7 2   You are West, with neither side
♡ K 3   vulnerable. South deals and passes.
♢ A Q J 7 5   You open 1♢ and your partner
♣ J 3   responds 1♡. What is your rebid?

Clearly, you must show your four-card major suit, with
a bid of 1♠. Your partner raises to 3♠ and you continue
to game.

The bidding: West   East
                    1♢   1♡
                    1♠   3♠
                    4♠

*North leads the ♣10 against West's contract of 4♠ and
South cashes ♣K and ♣A before switching to the ♡Q.
Plan the play.*

♠ K 10 7 2   ♠ Q 6 4 3
♡ K 3   ♡ A 9 6 5
♢ A Q J 7 5   ♢ K 10 6
♣ J 3   ♣ Q 7

Planning and play: Having lost two club tricks you can't
afford to lose more than one spade. As South has turned
up with nine points so far and did not open, it would be
reasonable to assume that North has the ♠A. Suppose
you win with the ♡K and lead a low spade to North's
♠8, East's ♠Q and South's ♠5. Now when you lead the
♠3 back, South plays the ♠9. What do you play from
the West hand?

Your best chance is simply to play low from your hand.
If North started with the doubleton ♠ A-8 your ♠K will
still be there to take care of South's ♠J.

3   Fit-finding Devices

To play with reasonable safety in a trump contract you need at least an eight-card fit (four in your hand, four in dummy or five in your hand and three in dummy, etc.) and your bidding must be capable of locating these combinations.

In the old days, when players held a hand with two four-card suits they would freely bid them both, to try to find a fit. The modern style is to bid two suits only if the hand is at least 5-4 shape or 4-4-4-1 shape. With two four-card suits it is better to open 1NT on a suitable point count, or to choose one of the suits for the opening bid and to rebid in no-trumps. If the two four-card suits are both majors and the point count is too strong for an opening 1NT, the correct opening bid is 1♡ and you rely on your partner to show a four-card spade suit if he has it.

In a bidding sequence, the bid of the fourth suit (e.g., 1♡ – 1♠, 2♣ – 2♢) is artificial and forcing. If responder genuinely had diamonds in this situation, his natural bid would be in no-trumps. The bid of the fourth suit demands further information, and should help the partnership to find the best fit.

Suppose you hold the hand shown on the right. Your partner opens 1♡ and you respond 1♠. If he rebids 2♣, you can bid the fourth suit, 2♢. His action will now depend on his shape and strength (see over).

♠ A Q 8 6 3
♡ A 3
♢ J 7 4
♣ 9 6 5

Hand A	*Hand B*	*Hand C*
♠ K 7 2	♠ J	♠ K 7
♡ K Q 10 7 5	♡ K Q J 7 5	♡ K Q J 10 9
◇ 5	◇ K Q 6	◇ 5 3
♣ K Q 7 2	♣ K Q 7 2	♣ A Q 4 2

The bidding:

1♡ – 1♠	1♡ – 1♠	1♡ – 1♠
2♣ – 2◇	2♣ – 2◇	2♣ – 2◇
3♠ – 4♠	3NT	3♡ – 4♡

In each case the partnership will have found the best spot. The bid of the fourth suit followed by agreement for opener's first suit, for example, 1♡ - 1♠, 2♣ - 2◇, 2NT - 3♡ is generally regarded as having created a forcing situation, allowing the partnership ample bidding space to explore the full possibilities of the hand.

Readers will be familiar with the fit-finding conventions that can be employed when one member of the partnership has opened in no-trumps. The most commonly played conventions are Stayman over 1NT and Baron over 2NT. Stayman explores for a fit in a major suit, whereas Baron explores a fit in either a major or a minor suit. If there is no fit in a Baron sequence, the partnership will usually subside in 3NT, so if a player makes a suit bid above the 3NT level, it is interpreted as a cue bid, agreeing the last-named suit. For example:

West	*East*
2NT (balanced, 20-22)	3♣ (Baron convention)
3◇	3♡
3♠	4♣ (cue bid, agreeing spades by inference)

If your partner opens 2NT and you have a five-card major, you can bid it, forcing him to choose between 3NT (if he has a doubleton in your suit) or to raise to

25

game if he has three or more. On the latter class of hand, since he is going to four of your major anyway, he might as well do some cue bidding on the way, to show you where he has controls. Thus in the sequence 2NT - 3♡, 4♣ opener is agreeing hearts by inference and showing first round control of clubs.

The play: In the play examples that follow, the planning of the hand to make the most of all one's chances, and the careful preservation of entries, are recurring features.

In addition, loser on loser plays are introduced. As the name suggests, the play consists of contributing a loser from both hands on the same trick. A simple example is shown below:

```
♠ —                         ♠ K Q 7 6
♡ A Q 10 7 5      N          ♡ K 3 2
♢ A Q 4        W     E       ♢ 5 3 2
♣ K Q 10 7 5      S          ♣ A J 6
```

West plays in 6♡ and it looks as if he has two diamond losers. However, he draws trumps and plays the ♠K from dummy, discarding a diamond on it (loser-on-loser). His other diamond loser goes away later on the established ♠Q.

```
♠ J 8 6 5        You are West, with neither side
♡ A K 3          vulnerable. You open 1NT and your
♢ 7 4 2          partner bids 2♣ (Stayman). You bid
♣ K Q 3          2♠ and your partner raises to 4♠.
```

26

North leads ♣J against West's contract of 4♠. Plan the play.

♠ J 8 6 5
♡ A K 3
◇ 7 4 2
♣ K Q 3

♠ A 7 4 2
♡ Q 5 2
◇ A Q 10 5
♣ 4 2

Planning and play: You are likely to lose a club and two spades, so you just have to be lucky in diamonds. Having drawn trumps, lead a diamond to the ◇10. If the finesse succeeds, return to your hand and lead towards the ◇ A-Q. North must hold both ◇K and ◇J for you to succeed.

♠ J 8 4
♡ A J 10 5 2
◇ 7 5
♣ 8 6 2

You are West, with neither side vulnerable. Your partner deals and opens 2NT. You respond 3♡ and he bids 4◇. What do you bid now?

There is absolutely no temptation to go beyond game. Your partner is limited, by his opening bid, to a maximum of 22 points, and although he has shown you first round control of diamonds, he has denied first round control of clubs. From your point of view 4♡ is quite enough, so that is what you bid.

The bidding:

West	East
	2NT
3♡	4◇ (cue bid, agreeing hearts)
4♡	

North leads the ♢Q against West's contract of 4♡. Plan the play.

```
♠ J 8 4              ┌─────────┐        ♠ A K 7
♡ A J 10 5 2         │    N    │        ♡ Q 4 3
♢ 7 5                │ W     E │        ♢ A K 8 3
♣ 8 6 2              │    S    │        ♣ K Q 7
                     └─────────┘
```

Planning and play: If the ♣A sits over dummy, you are likely to lose two clubs and a spade. In that case, you will have to hope that South has the ♡K. So, win the opening lead in dummy and lead the ♡3 towards your own hand, finessing the ♡10 if South plays low. If the ♡10 holds the trick, return to dummy with a spade to repeat the finesse.

Postscript: It's a mistake to lead the ♡Q from dummy. If South holds the singleton ♡K, you will have set up a winner in North's holding of ♡ 9-x-x-x.


```
♠ A 10 9 6       You are West, with North-South
♡ A K 2          vulnerable. You open 2NT and your
♢ J 4            partner responds 3♣. What do you
♣ A K Q 3        bid now?
```

Partner's bid of 3♣ is the Baron 3♣ convention asking you to show your biddable suits in ascending order. If your only four-card suit were clubs you would have to bid 3NT but on this hand you can show your spades cheaply by bidding 3♠. Over 3♠ partner bids 4♢. What do you do next?

Partner's 4♢ is a cue bid, agreeing your suit and guaranteeing first round control of diamonds. You are happy to co-operate by cue bidding your ace of hearts and your partner now bids 6♠.

The bidding:

	West	East
	2NT	3♣
	3♠	4♢
	4♡	6♠

North leads the ♠2 against West's contract of 6♠. Plan the play.

♠ A 10 9 6		♠ K Q J 7
♡ A K 2	N	♡ 8 7 6
♢ J 4	W E	♢ A 9 6 5 3
♣ A K Q 3	S	♣ 7

Planning and play: The spades are very solid but you have a possible loser in each of the other suits. However, it should be easy to make your contract by taking two ruffs in dummy.

Win the first trick with one of dummy's high trumps. Play the ♣7 to the ♣ A-K, discarding a heart from dummy. Ruff the ♣3 high. Return to ♡ A-K and now ruff a heart high. Come back to hand with a trump, draw the outstanding trumps and cash the last top club and the ♢A.

♠ K Q 8 6	You are East, dealer, with neither
♡ K J 7 2	side vulnerable. What is your opening
♢ A Q 8	bid on this hand?
♣ Q J	

You would like to open 1NT on this balanced hand but you are too strong. You must, therefore, bid a suit and rebid in no-trumps. With both major suits, you should open 1♡. Then you will not miss a heart or spade fit, as partner will respond 1♠ if he holds the suit. On this hand partner *does* bid 1♠, you raise to 3♠ and partner bids 4♠.

North leads the ♠9 against West's contract of 4♠. Plan the play from West's point of view.

♠ A 7 5 4		♠ K Q 8 6
♡ 9	N	♡ K J 7 2
◇ 10 7 6	W E	◇ A Q 8
♣ A 9 6 3 2	S	♣ Q J

Planning: Without the spade lead, West would have been able to ruff hearts in his own hand, but the opponents are sure to continue spades when they get in. Should West try to sneak a low heart to the ♡K, or should he finesse the ◇Q or try to set up the clubs? There are several choices of play on this hand.

Assuming that trumps split 3-2 (there is not much hope for the contract if they don't), West can count four spade tricks, maybe four clubs and hopefully two tricks in the red suits. The key to the hand will be to preserve entries to the West hand, so the first trick must be won in dummy.

Play: Win with the ♠K in dummy and lead the ♣Q. If this loses to North's ♣K and he returns a trump, win with dummy's ♠Q, cash ♣J, re-enter the West hand with a trump to the ace and cash the ♣A. If the clubs don't split (one of the opponents still has the ♣10) lead a fourth round of clubs and ruff with dummy's last trump. Exit from dummy with a heart, planning to ruff a heart later, cash the last club and finesse the ◇Q.

The full deal:

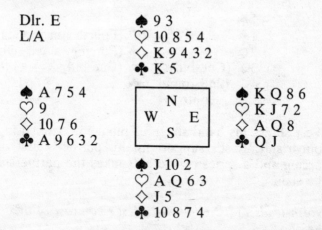

Dlr. E
L/A

♠ 9 3
♡ 10 8 5 4
◇ K 9 4 3 2
♣ K 5

♠ A 7 5 4
♡ 9
◇ 10 7 6
♣ A 9 6 3 2

W   E

♠ K Q 8 6
♡ K J 7 2
◇ A Q 8
♣ Q J

♠ J 10 2
♡ A Q 6 3
◇ J 5
♣ 10 8 7 4

Postscript: This awkward little hand sorted the men from the boys in a club duplicate event. For the contract to succeed one or two things have to be right, but even so, West has to keep a careful watch on his entries.

♠ K J 8 5 4
♡ A
◇ 10 4
♣ A Q J 4 2

You are West, dealer, with neither side vulnerable. What is your opening bid on this hand?

With two five-card black suits the classic opening bid is 1♣, planning to rebid twice in spades, hopefully whilst still at the two level.

The bidding:	*West*	*East*
	1♣	1♡
	1♠	2♢ (Fourth suit forcing)
	2♠	3♣ (Forcing, agrees clubs)
	3♡ (Cue bid)	3♠ (Cue bid)
	4♡ (2nd round control)	6♣

West shows his hand shape as planned. After using the fourth suit, East's support for his partner's first suit is forcing and a series of cue bids takes the partnership to the slam.

North leads the ♢K against West's contract of 6♣. Plan the play.

♠ K J 8 5 4		♠ A 3
♡ A	N	♡ 9 8 7 6 4
♢ 10 4	W E	♢ A 7
♣ A Q J 4 2	S	♣ K 8 6 3

Planning: You need time to set up your spade suit but that diamond lead is awkward as it exposes a weakness straight away. Perhaps you can set up your spades and get rid of your diamond at the same time. Yes, that's it . . . a loser on loser play.

The play: Win with the ♢A, cash ♠A and ♠K (hoping that both opponents follow) and then lead another spade, discarding ♢7 from dummy. If spades are 3-3 you are home. If they are 4-2 you will have to ruff another spade high in dummy next time. You will also have to take a diamond ruff in dummy to bring home your twelve tricks.

4 Finding the Fit in Competition

There is a special skill in finding the partnership fit in competitive situations. Just to remind you of some of the basics, when the opponents have started bidding and you want to get into the action, you have the following options:

(a) *To overcall in a suit:* This shows a good suit of five or more cards. The hand should contain at least four playing tricks if the overcall can be made at the one-level (e.g. 1♠ over 1♢), at least five playing tricks if the bid has to be made at the two level (e.g., 2♢ over 1♠). For example:

♠ 9 7 2	♠ K 7
♡ A Q J 10 3	♡ 8 3 2
♢ Q J 2	♢ A J 10 9 7 3
♣ 10 5	♣ K 6
Overcall 1♣ with 1♡	Overcall 1♠ with 2♢

(b) *To make a jump overcall:* This shows a very good suit of six or more cards and about 7 playing tricks.

♠ K Q J 10 8 4	♠ 8 3
♡ A 5 4	♡ K 8 3
♢ 5	♢ A K Q 9 7 4
♣ K Q 4	♣ A 7
Overcall 1♣, 1♢ or 1♡ with 2♠	Overcall 1♣ with 2♢, or one of a major with 3♢

33

(c) *To overcall in no-trumps:* This shows a balanced hand of 15–17 high card points and a good stop, preferably a double stop, in the opponent's suit.

♠ K J 5   Overcall any suit bid with 1NT
♡ A Q 6
♢ K J 6
♣ K 10 9 6

(d) *To bid the 'unusual no-trump':* This is normally an overcall of 2NT over the opponent's opening bid of one of a suit. Traditionally a 2NT overcall over the opponent's 1♡ or 1♠ showed a minor two suiter, at least 5-5 shape in clubs and diamonds, poor in defence but with some high cards in the minor suits. Nowadays its use has been extended to situations in which the opponents have opened in a minor suit. In each of these situations it shows the *two lowest unbid suits*. Over 1♣ it shows diamonds and hearts, over 1♢ it shows clubs and hearts.

♠ 7	♠ 6 2	♠ 5 2
♡ 4 2	♡ K J 9 5 3	♡ A J 10 7 3
♢ Q J 10 8 4	♢ 8	♢ K J 10 7 2
♣ K Q 10 4 2	♣ K Q J 8 3	♣ 9
Bid 2NT over 1♡	Bid 2NT over 1♢	Bid 2NT over 1♣

(e) *To make a take-out double:* The double of opponent's suit bid is basically for take-out, showing support for the other three suits.

(i)   ♠ K 8 6 3   (ii) ♠ K 6 3 2
      ♡ –   ♡ 8 5
      ◇ K J 8 5 2   ◇ A K 8 3
      ♣ Q J 10 4   ♣ K Q 6

Double 1♡ for take-out on either of these hands. They are about the same in playing strength.

However, in modern practice, the double can also be used to show three other types of hand, strong one-suiters, strong two-suiters and very strong balanced hands that are too good for a 1NT overcall. Strong one-suiters that are shown in this way should be too strong for a jump overcall, that is, they should contain 8-9 playing tricks, rather like an Acol opening 2-bid. Strong two-suiters should have much the same maximum strength but, because of the increased chance of finding a suit fit, a minimum of about seven tricks is acceptable. Strong balanced hands that are shown by first doubling should contain 18 points or more.

How does your partner recognise which hand type you hold? If you hold the traditional three-suited hand you will either raise his response or pass, according to your strength. If you hold the strong one-suiter you will bid your own suit over partner's response, if you hold the strong two-suiter you will cue bid the opponent's suit over his response, and if you hold the strong balanced hand you will bid no-trumps over his response.

Thus, on all the following hands, if the opponents open 1♡, you would double first. Let's assume partner responds 1♠.

♠ K Q 4 2	♠ 9 4	♠ 8	♠ K 10 3
♡ –	♡ A K 3	♡ 7 4	♡ A K 4
◇ A K 7 3	◇ K Q J 10 9 3	◇ K Q J 10 3	◇ K Q J 6
♣ K Q 5 3 2	♣ K Q	♣ A K Q 4 2	♣ A 4 3

Now bid 2♠	Now bid 2◇	Now bid 2♡	Now bid 1NT

Thus the double is a much more flexible bid than it once was, giving one the opportunity to describe a number of important hand types, without ambiguity.

(f) *To cue bid the opponent's suit:* This shows an extremely powerful and shapely hand that is unconditionally forcing to game. In the old days it would definitely show first or second round control of the opponent's suit, but now this would not be guaranteed.

♠ 8	♠ K Q J 10 4
♡ K Q J 10 6	♡ 6
◇ A K 6 3	◇ A K J 10 4 3
♣ A K J	♣ A
Bid 2♠ over opponent's 1♠	Bid 2♣ over opponent's 1♣
	Bid 2♡ over opponent's 1♡

There is an alternative use to which some players put the immediate cue bid of opponent's suit, and that is to show various types of weak two-suited hands. Readers who wish to find out more about these can look them up in text books under the titles of Michaels cue bids, or an alternative convention called Ghestem bids. As the unusual no-trump covers several of the possible weak two-suiters, we shall not go into these methods and will stick to the traditional use of the immediate cue bid of opponent's suit to show game-forcing hands. Both, however, are described in Rhoda Lederer's *Bridge Conventions Made Clear*.

(g) *To pass:* With a fairly balanced hand of moderate strength, up to about 15 points, you may have to pass if the opponents have opened the bidding before you.

♠ K 7 6
♡ K Q 7 3
♢ A 7 4
♣ Q 10 3

If opponents open the bidding you will have to pass. Your hand is unsuitable for any course of action (a) to (f) described above. It is a defensive, not an attacking hand, so don't make the mistake of thinking you must find a bid, just because you've got 14 points.

♠ K Q 10 9 3
♡ K 8 2
♢ 7 3 2
♣ K 4

You are West, with neither side vulnerable. Your right-hand opponent, South, opens 1♢. What do you bid?

If you play in your long suit, you should make three or four spade tricks and about one trick outside, so you have the qualifications for a one-level overcall. You, therefore, bid 1♠, and your partner raises you to 2♠. He is right to raise your suit with three to the ace (hand shown below) as you must have a good suit for your overcall. He is also right to raise only to the two-level with his eleven points, because a non-vulnerable one-level overcall will not have much in outside values.

Against 2♠ by West, North leads a diamond to his partner's ♢ A-K-Q. South now plays ♡A followed by ♡Q to West's ♡K. Plan the play.

♠ K Q 10 9 3
♡ K 8 2
♢ 7 3 2
♣ K 4

♠ A 4 2
♡ 7 6 3
♢ J 6 4
♣ A Q 9 8

Planning: You have lost four tricks in the red suits but you may be able to make all the remaining tricks if you play the trumps in the most efficient manner.

The play: Play the ♠K from your own hand, then a low spade to the ♠A. If North shows out on the second round you can successfully finesse against South's ♠J on the way back. If it's North who has four spades to the jack, you will lose a spade trick but you need not lose the contract. Simply cash the ♠K, ♠A and ♣Q and turn your attention to clubs. On the third club, discard your losing heart. If North ruffs, he gives up his natural trump trick.

♠ Q 10 6 4	You are West, with both sides vulner-
♡ 10 4 3	able. Your left-hand opponent, North,
◇ A 5 2	opens 1♡ and your partner doubles.
♣ K 6 5	South passes. What do you bid?

With no points at all you would be forced to respond 1♠, so with such a reasonable collection of cards it must be right to jump to 2♠ (non-forcing but showing 9+ points in response to the double). Your partner now bids 3♠ and you decide to try for game.

The bidding:	*West*	*North*	*East*	*South*
		1♡	Dbl	NB
	2♠	NB	3♠	NB
	4♠			

North leads the ♡ A-K against West's contract of 4♠, South playing the ♡8 followed by the ♡6. North continues with the ♡Q. Plan the play.

♠ Q 10 6 4	N	♠ A K 5 2
♡ 10 4 3	W E	♡ 5 2
◇ A 5 2	S	◇ K Q 10 6
♣ K 6 5		♣ A 8 2

Planning and play: It looks as if South started with a doubleton heart. If you ruff low in dummy, you will be over-ruffed. If you ruff high, you could lose a trump trick to the ♠ J-x-x later. The solution is to discard a club from dummy, another example of a loser-on-loser play. Now, if trumps break reasonably, you should be safe, as you will be able to ruff your third club in dummy at a later stage.

♠ 7 2	You are West, not vulnerable against
♡ K J 10 6 5 2	vulnerable opponents. North opens
◇ 5	1♠, your partner doubles and South
♣ 9 8 7 4	bids 2♠. What do you bid?

When a player makes a take-out double of a major suit, he usually has support for the other major, so a good fit is almost guaranteed. With such a shapely hand you are worth one shot, and you should bid 3♡.

Now partner bids 3NT, revealing that his hand is the very strong, balanced variety, 18 points or more.

Obviously you can't stand 3NT on your hand so you must retreat to 4♡.

The bidding:

West	North	East	South
	1♠	Dbl	2♠
3♡	NB	3NT	NB
4♡			

North leads the ♠Q against West's contract of 4♡. Plan the play.

♠ 7 2		♠ A K 9
♡ K J 10 6 5 2	N	♡ A Q 9
◇ 5	W E	◇ A 7 6 2
♣ 9 8 7 4	S	♣ Q 5 3

Planning and play: Although dummy has good high cards, there are no ruffing values, and West can see only nine tricks on top. But dummy's trumps are strong, and *they* can be used to draw the opponent's trumps whilst all the ruffs are taken in the West hand, a classic dummy reversal play.

Win the lead, play the other top spade and ruff a spade. Go over to the ♢A and ruff a diamond high. Play a low trump to the ♡9, ruff a second diamond high. play a low trump to the ♡Q and ruff a third diamond high. Now dummy is left with the ♡A and just three losing clubs.

♠ A Q 3	You are West, with neither
♡ –	side vulnerable. Your right
♢ A K Q J 10 9 8 7	hand opponent opens 1♡.
♣ A 5	What do you bid?

With such an exceptional hand containing 10½ playing tricks, you must do something special, so you must start with a cue bid of the opponent's suit. Over 2♡ from you, partner responds 3♣ and you jump to 4♢ (a jump bid in a forcing situation) to show your solid diamond suit. With no points at all partner would have to keep the bidding open now, so on his actual hand (shown on p. 41), containing an ace and a queen he raises you to 6♢.

The bidding:	West	North	East	South
				1♡
	2♡	NB	3♣	NB
	4♢	NB	6♢	

North leads a trump against West's contract of 6♢. Plan the play.

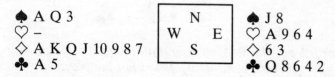

♠ A Q 3
♡ –
♢ A K Q J 10 9 8 7
♣ A 5

♠ J 8
♡ A 9 6 4
♢ 6 3
♣ Q 8 6 4 2

Planning and play: West is forced to take the trump lead in his own hand. There is no easy entry to dummy so it looks as if West must lose a spade and a club if he can't get to dummy's ♡A for a discard.

It won't work to play ♠A and another, hoping to get to dummy with a spade ruff, because the defence will draw dummy's last trump when they win with the ♠K. The solution is to play the ♠Q. If the opponents win with the ♠K, the ♠J will provide an entry to dummy. If they duck the ♠Q, West can continue with ♠A and a spade ruff, then discard a club on the ♡A.

♠ 10 8 4
♡ Q 6 4
♢ 10
♣ K Q J 6 4 2

You are West, with neither side vulnerable. North opens 1♡ and your partner doubles. What do you respond when South passes?

For the moment you must take it that partner has a three-suited hand and is asking you to choose the suit. As you would be forced to bid 2♣ with no points at all, you must jump to 3♣ on this reasonable hand. Over 3♣ your partner bids 3♡. What do you do now?

Partner has doubled first, then cue bid the opponent's suit. This sequence shows a strong two-suiter in the unbid suits, spades and diamonds. You must, therefore, forget about your clubs and agree one of your partner's suits by bidding 3♠, which partner raises to 4♠.

The bidding:	West	North	East	South
		1♡	Dbl	NB
	3♣	NB	3♡	NB
	3♠	NB	4♠	

North leads the ♠A and continues with the ♠2 against West's contract of 4♠. Plan the play.

♠ 10 8 4		♠ K Q J 9 6
♡ Q 6 4	N	♡ A
◇ 10	W E	◇ A K 8 6 4 2
♣ K Q J 6 4 2	S	♣ 9

Planning: It seems strange to be playing 4♠ from your side of the table. Now that spades have been led, you can only get one diamond ruff in the West hand. You must set up one of the long minor suits, and the choice has to be diamonds, because the East hand holds most of the entries.

The play: Win the second spade trick. Play ◇A and a low diamond, ruffing with the last spade. Enter dummy with the ♡A, draw the last trump and cash the ◇K. If the diamonds don't split 3-3, simply give up a diamond to establish the suit.

Postscript: The contract will fail if the diamonds are 5-1 or 6-0. The trump lead cut down your ability to ruff in the short-trump hand.

♠ A 10 2	You are West, with neither side
♡ K Q 7	vulnerable. Your right hand opponent
◇ Q J 5	opens 1♡. What do you bid?
♣ A K 5 3	

You are balanced and strong, with a good stop in the opponent's suit but you are too strong for a simple over-call of 1NT. Thus, you must double first and bid no-trumps later. Over your double, North passes and your partner bids 2◇. You now bid 2NT and your partner goes on to 3NT.

The bidding:

West	North	East	South
			1♡
Dbl	NB	2◇	NB
2NT	NB	3NT	

North ignores his partner's suit and leads the ♠6 against West's contract of 3NT. Dummy's ♠9 is played and South follows with the ♠3. Plan the play.

♠ A 10 2		♠ Q J 9
♡ K Q 7	N	♡ 8 6 4
◇ Q J 5	W E	◇ K 10 7 6 4
♣ A K 5 3	S	♣ J 2

Planning: Partner's raise to 3NT is justified on seven points and a five-card suit, but there is quite a lot of work to do. You will have to set up the diamonds, and if the opponents hold up the ◇A you will need an outside entry to the dummy.

The play: Overtake the ♠9 with the ♠A. Play ◇Q, ◇J and another to force out the ◇A. The ♠Q or the ♠J will now be a sure entry to dummy when you regain the lead. Now you can run the diamonds and play on hearts.

Postscript: If you are greedy and play a low spade from your own hand on the first trick, North can always block your entry to dummy. Thus if you lead a low spade from your remaining ♠ A-10 he will put in the ♠K immediately and your ♠A will block the suit; if you play ♠A and then ♠10 he will win the third round of the suit.

♠ Q 9 8 7 5
♡ K Q 10 5
◇ J 8 5
♣ 7

You are West, with your side vulnerable. Your left-hand opponent, North, opens 1♣ and your partner bids 2NT. South bids 4♣. What do you do?

Partner's 2NT overcall is the unusual no-trump, showing the two lowest unbid suits, diamonds and hearts. Although East's hand will not be strong, it will have 5-5 or better shape. It is very unlikely that you will defend successfully against 4♣. With good support for hearts and a reasonable fit for diamonds, the partnership hands are fitting well, and it is worth trying 4♡.

The bidding:

West	North	East	South
	1♣	2NT	4♣
4♡	All pass		

Against West's contract of 4♡, North leads the ◇7 to the ◇A, ◇6 and ◇5. Plan the play.

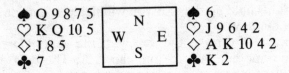

♠ Q 9 8 7 5   ♠ 6
♡ K Q 10 5   ♡ J 9 6 4 2
◇ J 8 5   ◇ A K 10 4 2
♣ 7   ♣ K 2

Planning: You can't afford to finesse the diamonds on the first round because you have to lose three aces. You might try to lead a club towards dummy's ♣K early in the play; if North has the ♣A he will have to play it (or not make a club trick). Then your ♣K will provide a discard for your losing diamond.

The play: Win the first trick with the ♢A and lead a low heart to your ♡K; if this wins the trick, try the club finesse. However, suppose North wins the second trick with the ♡A and leads the ♢9. Now you should recognise North's play of the diamond suit as MUD (middle-up-down), and put up dummy's ♢K, to drop South's ♢Q.

5 Countering the Opponents' Fit-finding Manoeuvres

In the last chapter we saw what good use a partnership can make of the double of a suit bid in a competitive auction. In this chapter we shall look at the counter-measures that are available to the opening side.

Action when opponents have doubled

Firstly, many responses are changed after an opponent has intervened with a double. For example, if partner opens 1♡ and the next hand doubles you should stretch if you have good trump support, to keep doubler's partner out of the bidding. If you have good trump support and good enough outside values to go to the three-level at least, it is standard practice to bid 2NT, to distinguish your hand from the stretched raise. If you are strong in outside values, then you redouble.

For example after 1♡ – Double:

♠ 9 2	♠ 9 2	♠ K 7	♠ K 9 6
♡ K 10 6 2	♡ K J 9 7 5	♡ K J 7 4	♡ K 9 6
♢ J 9 8	♢ K 9 5	♢ K 9 6 4	♢ K 9 6 4
♣ 8 7 5 4	♣ 8 6 4	♣ 9 7 5	♣ Q 10 3
Stretch to	Stretch to	Bid 2NT	Redouble
2♡	3♡	(a sound 3♡)	

The redouble announces good values (9 plus points) without 4-card support for partner's suit. It is primarily a statement that your side has the balance of points and you are ready to punish the opponents if they get too high. However, redoubling sequences can often go wrong if both members of the partnership don't co-operate. It's up to the opener to warn his partner off if he has opened on a weak distributional hand, or to co-operate in doubling the opponents if it looks as if it is better to defend.

For example, you open 1♠, next hand doubles, partner redoubles and the doubler's partner bids 2♢.

(a)	(b)	(c)	(d)
♠ K 8 7 4 3	♠ K Q 10 9 7 4	♠ K Q 7 5 4	♠ K Q 7 5
♡ A Q 10 8 5	♡ A 7 4	♡ A 7 6	♡ A 7 6
♢ J 4	♢ J 4	♢ 6 5	♢ K Q 7
♣ 8	♣ 7 5	♣ A Q 8	♣ J 7 5

Bid 2♡ on hand (a) and 2♠ on hand (b); you don't want partner to go doubling 2♢ when you have such poor defence. Pass on hand (c); you have nothing to be ashamed of but it's best to leave the decision to partner. Double on hand (d), where defence to 2♢ seems attractive.

Judging the level

Another particular difficulty in competitive sequences is to judge how high to go, as you are often unsure if partner is bidding soundly or merely competing for the contract. It is good practice to stretch only if the hands appear to be fitting well, and to hold back if you have any serious doubts. The corollary is that if partner is 'pushing the boat out' in a competitive sequence, you should be able to rely on him for some degree of fit for your suit. For example, if you open 1♠, your opponent overcalls with 2♡ and your partner bids 3♣, you know that your partner has an excellent club suit and enough points to play in a three-level contract, but it is also likely that he has at least tolerance for your spades. If he hates your spades he should not be leading you on. He should simply sit back and let the opponents struggle with a misfitting hand.

If, after a competitive auction, you have reached the three-level and are wondering whether to go on to game, you will often come to the right answer by thinking back to what partner did, or did not do, at an earlier round of the bidding, so just take a moment or two to think the whole sequence through.

Making them pay

You may have the opportunity to double the opponents for penalties after a competitive sequence in which they have got too high. However, always bid as high as you dare in your own or partner's suit, before you try a penalty double of the opponent's contract. Remember that the more cards you hold in your partner's suit (and he in yours) the less losers the opponents have in these suits.

A penalty double of any low-level contract is always an expression of opinion, rather than a command, and doubler's partner should feel free to take it out if his hand is unsuitable for defence.

For example, if you open 1♠, your left-hand opponent bids 2♦ and your partner doubles for penalties:

(a)♠ Q J 9 6 3 2   (b)♠ A 10 7 6 2   (c)♠ A 10 7 6 2
♡ K Q 9 5   ♡ K Q 9   ♡ A K 9
♦ –   ♦ 8 7   ♦ 8
♣ K J 6   ♣ K J 7   ♣ K Q 4 2

Bid 2♡ on hand (a); your diamond void and lack of quick tricks make it most unsuitable for defence. Pass on hand (b); although you have only average values, you do have two trumps, so overcaller's partner is likely to be short of them. Pass on hand (c); although you have only one trump you have four quick tricks and can look forward to a profitable defence.

Defence to transfer bids

Transfer bids are becoming very popular, and although we are not going to advocate their use in this book, it is necessary to know something about them, so that one can plan an effective defence.

The most common transfer bids are the so-called 'red-suit transfers' in response to 1NT (or 2NT). In their simplest form, a response of 2♦ over 1NT demands a transfer to 2♡ and a response of 2♡ demands a transfer to 2♠. For example:

♠ K 10 3   ┌─────────┐   ♠ 7 5
♡ A J 4   │   N   │   ♡ Q 9 7 3 2
♦ Q 10 4   │ W   E │   ♦ 9 6 2
♣ K 10 6 2   │   S   │   ♣ 7 5 3
                  └─────────┘

The bidding will go 1NT-2♦, 2♡-NB. Thus responder

bids the transfer suit (diamonds) and opener transfers to the destination suit (hearts). The idea is to get the contract played by the stronger, opening hand with the lead coming up to its high cards.

The transfer bid also acts as a 'master switch' to set the bidding on a new course. Thus, every sequence following a transfer bid can be given a particular meaning, so the language of bidding is enriched. There are plenty of books that give a good description of transfer bids and we are not going to go into details here. We will just describe a simple defence.

(a) Although many players use the double of a transfer response to 1NT to show a strong, balanced hand of the type that would have doubled 1NT, the principle given elsewhere in the book is that a double of an artificial bid should show the suit, so we will stick to that method here. Thus **the double of a transfer bid shows a good holding in that suit**. For example:

If your left-hand opponent opens 1NT and your right-hand opponent responds 2♡ (as a transfer bid) double to ensure a heart lead.	♠ 6 3 2 ♡ K Q J 7 3 ◇ J 7 6 ♣ K 8

(b) **The bid of the opponent's destination suit is for take-out**, showing support for the other three suits.

Dlr. W
L/A

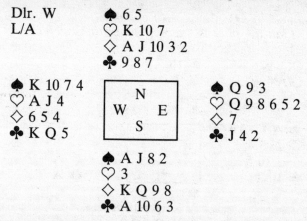

♠ 6 5
♡ K 10 7
♢ A J 10 3 2
♣ 9 8 7

♠ K 10 7 4
♡ A J 4
♢ 6 5 4
♣ K Q 5

♠ Q 9 3
♡ Q 9 8 6 5 2
♢ 7
♣ J 4 2

♠ A J 8 2
♡ 3
♢ K Q 9 8
♣ A 10 6 3

In this hand from a teams-of-four match, West opened
1NT and East bid 2◇ as a transfer to 2♡. South now bid
2♡, the destination suit, as a take-out manoeuvre and
found the excellent diamond part-score.

Making the most of the play

Again, in the examples of card play that follow, we shall
see the importance of correct suit handling, particularly
in the play of the trump suit.

We shall also see some further examples of loser-on-
loser play. The immense power of this technique is dem-
onstrated in the following deal.

West plays in 4♠ after North has pre-empted in clubs.
Plan the play to succeed against any defence.

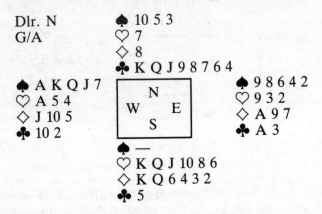

Dlr. N
G/A

♠ 10 5 3
♡ 7
◇ 8
♣ K Q J 9 8 7 6 4

♠ A K Q J 7
♡ A 5 4
◇ J 10 5
♣ 10 2

♠ 9 8 6 4 2
♡ 9 3 2
◇ A 9 7
♣ A 3

♠ —
♡ K Q J 10 8 6
◇ K Q 6 4 3 2
♣ 5

Planning: Although East has a good trump fit, his shape exactly mirrors West's, and there seems to be no chance of ruffing in dummy. At first sight, therefore, there appear to be only 8 top tricks. However, there is one way of being 100% sure of making the contract. Try to work it out before looking at the answer, set out below.

The play: Win the first trick with the ace of whichever suit North leads. Draw trumps, cash the remaining aces and throw North into the lead with a club. You are now down to the following cards:

♠ J 7
♡ 5 4
◇ J 10
♣ —

♠ 9 8
♡ 9 3
◇ 9 7
♣ —

At this stage it still looks as if there are four losers in the red suits but North has only clubs to lead. You could ruff his club lead in one hand and discard a loser from the other hand, so reducing your losers to three, but a much better plan is to discard a loser from each hand, say a heart from East and a diamond from West. Poor North is still on lead and forced to lead another club, on which you discard dummy's last heart and your own last diamond. Now you can cross-ruff the hand, having reduced four red suit losers to two.

♠ A K 5 ♡ K 9 8 3 2 ◇ J 2 ♣ K 9 3	You are West, with neither side vulnerable, and you open 1♡. North doubles and your partner raises you to 3♡. South passes. What should you bid?

You must remember that, after a take-out double, many responses by opener's partner are changed. If East had had a sound raise to 3♡ he would have bid 2NT in this situation. His direct raise to 3♡ shows good heart support but is pre-emptive, and you should not be tempted to bid on. You, therefore, pass, and 3♡ becomes the final contract.

The bidding:

West	North	East	South
1♡	Dbl	3♡	All pass

North leads the ♡5 against West's contract of 3♡. Plan the play.

♠ A K 5		♠ 9 7 6
♡ K 9 8 3 2	N	♡ A Q 10 7 6
◇ J 2	W　　E	◇ 10 9
♣ K 9 3	S	♣ Q 10 6

Planning: The opponent's heart lead has not helped you. It looks as though you may lose one spade, two diamonds and two clubs. However, if the opponents can be made to lead the clubs themselves you will escape with one club loser.

The play: Win the opening lead and draw the remaining trumps. Play off the ♠A and ♠K and exit with the ♠5. The opponents will cash their ♠Q and two diamonds, but will be forced then either to continue with a spade or diamond, giving you a ruff and discard, or to open up the clubs, allowing you to make two tricks in the suit.

♠ 10 9 8 4 3	You are East, with East-West vulner-
♡ 3	able. Your partner, West, deals and
♢ A J 8 4 3	opens 1♠. North doubles. What do
♣ 10 3	you bid?

With such a good fit for partner's suit you should raise him to the limit. There is a real risk that the opponents have a heart contract and you should do your best to pre-empt them with a bid of 4♠. This concludes the auction and North is on lead. Now let's move over to look at the hand from West's point of view.

North leads the ♣K against West's contract of 4♠. Plan the play.

♠ Q J 7 6 2		♠ 10 9 8 4 3
♡ A Q J 10 9	N	♡ 3
♢ –	W E	♢ A J 8 4 3
♣ A 8 6	S	♣ 10 3

Planning: With two trumps to lose, West must restrict himself to one loser in the side suits, so he can't afford to lose a heart and a club. One loser must be ditched somewhere and this can be done by way of a 'loser-on-loser' play.

The play: West should win the first club trick and immediately play ♡A followed by ♡Q from his hand. Whether or not North plays the ♡K, the losing club is thrown from dummy. If North does win and continues hearts, dummy must ruff high to prevent South from over-ruffing with a low trump. There are alternative ways of playing the hand, but the contract should be safe on the simple line suggested.

♠ A Q
♡ 9 3
◇ A K 10 7 4 2
♣ Q 7 4

You are West, with both sides vulnerable. You open 1◇, North overcalls with 2♣ and your partner responds 2♡. You rebid 3◇ and your partner bids 3♡. What do you do now?

When the hand was played in a teams event, the bidding at one table went:

West	North	East	South
1◇	2♣	2♡	NB
3◇	NB	3♡	All pass

and East-West missed a vulnerable game.

West claimed that he did not know how many hearts his partner had and could not realise that he was so strong. However, he had missed the point. To insist on hearts to this degree must surely show six, or a completely solid five-card suit. What strength was East showing? When he bid 2♡ he was prepared to go to the three level over a minimum rebid from West. He, therefore, must have at least ten or eleven points and West should bid 4♡ with confidence.

The full deal:

♠ A Q
♡ 9 3
◇ A K 10 7 4 2
♣ Q 7 4

W N E S

♠ K J 3
♡ A Q 10 7 4 2
◇ J 5 3
♣ 6

In practice West lost only one heart and one club.

Of course, it would have been much easier if the opponents had not intervened, for the bidding would then have gone 1◇-1♡, 2◇-3♡ and West would have had no difficulty in going on to 4♡. In these competitive sequences one has to trust one's partner. If East were weaker he would not have bid 2♡ over North's 2♣, if his hearts had been worse he would have let West play in diamonds. If he thought the hand had misfitting features he would not be bidding so bravely, so some sort of fit for West's diamond suit is almost guaranteed. This hand is a good illustration – East could hardly have less than this, yet the contract makes with an overtrick.

♠ K J 10 6 2	You are West, with neither side
♡ 6 2	vulnerable. Your partner opens 1◇.
◇ Q 5 4	What do you bid if South intervenes
♣ A 9 6	with (a) 1♡ or (b) 2NT?

Over 1♡ there is no problem. You simply ignore the interference and respond 1♠, so the bidding takes an unimpeded course. Over 2NT there is a problem. The 2NT overcall is the unusual 2NT, showing the two lowest unbid suits, clubs and hearts. The trouble is that, to show your suit, you have to bid 3♠, and if East doesn't like this, he may have to go to the four-level.

In such cases you have to balance possible losses against possible gains. The possible gain is a game, in spades perhaps, your way. What is the worst that can happen? Well, if partner opened on a reasonably balanced hand, he must have 15 points or more (or he would have opened 1NT) and he is likely to have at least a semi-fit for your spades. If, on the other hand, he is weak and distributional, he will rebid 4◇ and, although you may be over the top, your ◇ Q-5-4 will be excellent support, and the opponents will not have an obvious double.

The full deal:

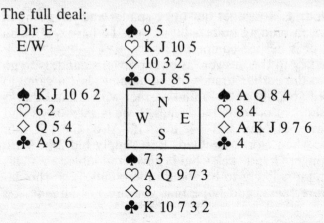

```
Dlr E              ♠ 9 5
E/W                ♡ K J 10 5
                   ◇ 10 3 2
                   ♣ Q J 8 5
♠ K J 10 6 2                        ♠ A Q 8 4
♡ 6 2          N                    ♡ 8 4
◇ Q 5 4      W   E                  ◇ A K J 9 7 6
♣ A 9 6          S                  ♣ 4
                   ♠ 7 3
                   ♡ A Q 9 7 3
                   ◇ 8
                   ♣ K 10 7 3 2
```

So the bidding should go:

West	North	East	South
		1◇	2NT
3♠	NB or 4♡	4♠	

But what if West's hearts and diamonds were reversed? Of course, the chances of finding a spade fit would be the same but to bid 3♠ is much less attractive now because of the danger of partner retreating to his own suit and getting doubled.

```
♠ K 10 8 4 2        With neither side vulnerable you,
♡ Q 10 8 7 3        West, deal this hand, and open
◇ A                 1♠. The next hand doubles and
♣ A 4               the bidding proceeds as shown
                    below:
```

West	North	East	South
1♠	Dbl	2♣	2◇
2♡	3◇	3♠	NB
?			

Do you go on to 4♠?

It sounds as if partner has three spades and he seems to have been bidding quite a bit so does he have a goodish hand, or is he just competing?

The key to the answer, as on a previous hand, is to go back to the earlier rounds of the bidding. For a game to succeed you will need to find partner with a hand that is little short of opening bid values. If he is as good as that he may well have bid 4♠ himself. Also, most significantly, when North doubled, East simply bid 2♣. With a stronger hand he would have redoubled, so his maximum is likely to be about nine points. You should, therefore, pass, and hope that you are not already too high.

North leads the ♢3 against West's contract of 3♠. Plan the play.

♠ K 10 8 4 2		♠ A 9 3
♡ Q 10 8 7 3	N	♡ 6 4
♢ A	W E	♢ J 2
♣ A 4	S	♣ Q J 10 9 6 3

Planning: You need to set up dummy's clubs but you are short of entries to the East hand. You will have to hope that the black suits break reasonably and you will also have to be careful to keep control of the trumps.

The play: After winning the first trick, probably your best chance is to play ♣A and another club. When you tackle trumps, play the ♠K and then the ♠A. Then run the clubs; if an opponent ruffs, the ♠9 will be an entry to the dummy.

6   Recognising the Misfit
Part 1   Uncontested
Sequences

It is exciting to keep playing for absolute tops, and if your name is Zia Mahmood this is undoubtedly winning bridge. For more ordinary mortals, however, playing for tops has the distressing side-effect of producing bottoms as well, and a more profitable line is to keep aiming for fair results whilst trying to avoid the disasters.

Most bridge wounds are self-inflicted and it is the bad boards that ruin our chances. Six or seven out of ten on each hand is World Championship stuff, as almost all large pairs events are won with a score of 65% or less. At rubber bridge the arithmetic is not so clearly defined but a few disasters wreak havoc with one's score, and with partnership confidence.

The disasters tend to occur on the misfits. Although it is stated that only about 15% of partnership hands have no suit fit, these are the ones you will remember. Also, there are a number of hands where you can't locate your fit, and play in an inferior contract.

It will help to avoid the disasters if you plan ahead in the bidding by asking yourself what is likely to happen on the next round of the auction. It will also pay you to be sensitive to situations that appear to indicate a misfit; on some of the following hands, you may consider that we have been extreme in recommending you to drop the

Fits and Misfits

bidding when you smell a misfit. Perhaps we have, but we want to illustrate the point.

1. Look for the cloud on the horizon.
For example, you hold the hand shown on the right and your partner opens 1♠. It's always bad news when partner bids your short suit. True, you may find a fit in one of your four-card suits later, but the bidding has started badly and you will have to be careful not to get too high.

♠ 7
♡ Q 10 7 2
♢ A 9 6 5
♣ J 10 7 2

Similarly, the warning bells should start to ring if partner responds in your short suit. You open 1♢ and begin to think about a slam if partner responds 1♠ or 2♣, but have no such ambitions if he responds 1♡.

♠ K 10 6
♡ –
♢ A K Q J 5 4
♣ A J 9 4

Again, with the hand shown, your spirits should sink a bit if your left-hand opponent opens 1♣, as then you will know the cards are sitting badly for you.

2. Don't insist on your rights on a misfit.
For example, if you hold the hand shown here and the bidding goes 1♡-1♠, 2♡-2♠, then give up! You may not be in the right spot but one of you has to give in.

♠ –
♡ A J 10 7 5 3
♢ 8 6 4 3
♣ A K 6

3. Avoid leaving a reasonable spot in favour of a questionable one.
Compare the three uncontested sequences shown below:

(a) West	East		(b) West	East		(c) West	East
1♢	1♠		1♢	1♠		1♢	1♠
1NT	2♠		2♢	2♠		2♣	2♠

In (a) opener won't have four spades but of the nine cards unaccounted for, three could be spades in a balanced hand. It's unlikely he has less than two or surely he would not rebid 1NT. Responder could pass 1NT if he wished but he need not feel too worried about bidding 2♠ because his partner should have at least a semi-fit. Also, since he has shown his points and shape exactly, West will accept East's decision and the bidding will not go on, getting out-of-hand.

Sequence (b) shows five diamonds, maybe six. If opener had a shapely hand and limited values he would have tried to support spades if he could, so maybe he is short of spades, and responder should think twice before insisting on his suit.

When the bidding goes 1◇-1♠-2♣ as in (c), opener should have at least 5-4 shape. Opener cannot be 2-3-4-4 or 3-2-4-4 or he would have opened 1NT on 12-14, or rebid 1NT if stronger. He cannot be 4-1-4-4 or he would have raised the spades. He can have at most four cards in the major suits. West has offered two suits and East should give serious consideration to agreeing to one of them as the trump suit. Of course, if East has seven spades or even six good ones, he has some insurance for a 2♠ bid, but he should be careful not to insist on spades with a five-card suit, or even a poor six-card suit and a minimum hand. He may be hitting his partner's void. Whilst there is certainly much truth in the argument that the contract is best played in the trump suit of the *weak* hand, because this is the only way to obtain entries to it, the argument can be taken too far. In the part-score situations that we are considering, it is better to accept the safety of a reasonable fit, even at duplicate pairs, than to strive for a higher score that may result in a ridiculous contract.

Here is a hand from a recent competition, that illustrates the point:

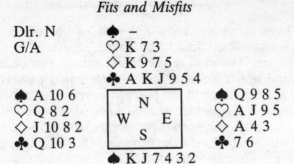

Dlr. N
G/A

♠ –
♡ K 7 3
♢ K 9 7 5
♣ A K J 9 5 4

♠ A 10 6
♡ Q 8 2
♢ J 10 8 2
♣ Q 10 3

♠ Q 9 8 5
♡ A J 9 5
♢ A 4 3
♣ 7 6

♠ K J 7 4 3 2
♡ 10 6 4
♢ Q 6
♣ 8 2

The bidding started 1♣ - 1♠, 2♣ and then South must have rebid 2♠ at nearly every table. As a result, a common score was 2♠-1 or -1 by South, and 3♣-1 occurred several times. Pairs who really did not know how to stop finished in 3♠ or even 4♣ going well down, of course.

Although it is very tempting to repeat your spades on the South hand, it can't be good practice in the long run when there is no future in going on. Thus a rebid of 2♠ in this situation should be reserved for hands which have game prospects if a suitable denomination can be found, not as an attempt to rescue partner from what you regard as an unsatisfactory contract. On the actual South hand it is better to pass; you may not be in the best spot but you are likely to have seven or eight clubs between you and you are not in a bizarre contract. If *you* make the mistake of bidding 2♠, it is even more vital for your partner to pass. One of you has to give up, and the sooner the better. If you can discipline yourself to stop in 2♣, things will not be too bad. East has a difficult lead and may well give declarer a trick. Now, if declarer can get into dummy to take the club finesse, he will come to eight tricks, the only positive score for North-South.

4. If partner responds 1NT to your opening suit bid, think twice before rebidding your suit.

Partner's 1NT response is usually made on a reasonably balanced hand of about 6-9 points. However, he is sometimes forced to respond 1NT on hands that fit your suit badly. For example, in a recent survey conducted by Eric Crowhurst for Bridge International, 92% of bridge experts said they would respond 1NT to their partner's opening 1♡ on ♠ K 4 2, ♡ 2, ◇ Q 10 7 5 2, ♣ K 8 7 3. Thus, if opener has a *reasonably* balanced collection, even with five hearts, he will be well advised to pass. 1NT will be playable but 2♡ could be murdered. This is a very modern style, so be sure you and your partner are on the same wavelength before plunging in too deep.

We are now about to move into a higher gear. Many of the hands that follow are taken from tournaments, and provide plenty of problems in the bidding, as well as in the play.

♠ K 8 4	You are East, with both sides vulner-
♡ K 10 8 4 3 2	able. After three passes your partner,
◇ J 9 3	West, opens 1♣. You respond 1♡,
♣ J	and he rebids 1♠. What do you bid now?

When partner has offered you two suits, you need to think twice before rejecting them both. You know that the hand has misfitting features when partner opens 1♣, so you don't wish to get too high. Thus, there is much to be said for passing 1♠. You are at least at a low level, so nothing too disastrous can happen and you may be able to make a couple of club ruffs in your hand to bring the contract home. If you rebid your hearts, you have to make eight tricks and, as partner has bid both black suits, he will be short of red cards. Obviously you are reluctant to pass partner's rebid as he may be quite strong but common sense should tell you this is not a game-going hand.

The full deal:

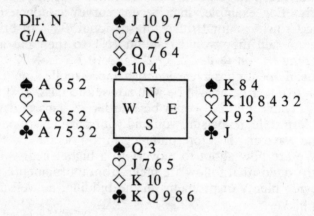

Dlr. N
G/A

♠ J 10 9 7
♡ A Q 9
◇ Q 7 6 4
♣ 10 4

♠ A 6 5 2
♡ –
◇ A 8 5 2
♣ A 7 5 3 2

♠ K 8 4
♡ K 10 8 4 3 2
◇ J 9 3
♣ J

♠ Q 3
♡ J 7 6 5
◇ K 10
♣ K Q 9 8 6

With twelve points and four spades, West was justified in entering the bidding as fourth player and, provided he stops in 1♠ he is likely to emerge with a positive score. In 2♡ there would be altogether too much work to do. Are there any circumstances in which East should definitely insist on his hearts? Yes, if his suit were much more solid but lacking the tops, such as ♡ Q-J-10-9-3-2. Now 2♡ will become comparatively much better; the heart holding will probably make four tricks in a heart contract but make no tricks in a spade contract, because of lack of entries.

♠ K Q J 7 2
♡ J 4 2
◇ 8 4
♣ 10 3 2

You are North, with neither side vulnerable. Your partner opens 1◇ and you respond 1♠. Partner's rebid is 2◇. What do you bid now?

Recognising the Misfit

As explained on p. 62, responder's rebid of his own suit
is normally interpreted as a constructive bid, suggesting
a possible game in his suit, opener's suit or no-trumps.
Clearly you are not strong enough to bid 2♠ construc-
tively with only seven points so, on the present hand, you
should pass. However, even if your partnership favours
the outmoded style of repeating responder's suit to sign
off, it would be unwise to do so on this hand. You know
that you have at least seven diamonds between you, and
you may have more, so 2◇ can't be unreasonable. If you
repeat your suit, you could easily run into a shortage of
spades in partner's hand, which would make 2♠ a ridiculous contract. Settle, therefore, for the substance of a
reasonable contract instead of the shadow of a possible
better contract, and pass.

The full deal:

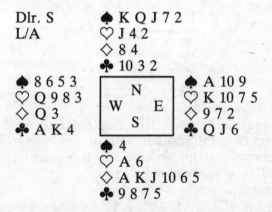

```
Dlr. S        ♠ K Q J 7 2
L/A           ♡ J 4 2
              ◇ 8 4
              ♣ 10 3 2
♠ 8 6 5 3              ♠ A 10 9
♡ Q 9 8 3      N       ♡ K 10 7 5
◇ Q 3      W     E     ◇ 9 7 2
♣ A K 4        S       ♣ Q J 6
              ♠ 4
              ♡ A 6
              ◇ A K J 10 6 5
              ♣ 9 8 7 5
```

In 2◇, since there is no entry to dummy, South will be
forced to play the diamonds from the top, and will scrape
home with six diamond tricks, one heart and (eventually)
one club. In 2♠ the defence will make two spades, at
least one heart and three clubs, so North will have some
explaining to do to his partner.

Postscript: If North's spades had been a little more solid, for example ♠ K-Q-J-10-2, he would have had a chance of making, if the opponents failed to find a heart lead. On the other hand, if his spades were more gappy, for example ♠ K-Q-10-7-2, his task would have been quite hopeless.

Consider the possible results of different bidding sequences on the North-South hands shown below:

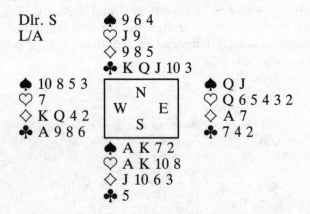

```
Dlr. S        ♠ 9 6 4
L/A           ♡ J 9
              ◇ 9 8 5
              ♣ K Q J 10 3
♠ 10 8 5 3        N        ♠ Q J
♡ 7                        ♡ Q 6 5 4 3 2
◇ K Q 4 2    W       E     ◇ A 7
♣ A 9 8 6         S        ♣ 7 4 2
              ♠ A K 7 2
              ♡ A K 10 8
              ◇ J 10 6 3
              ♣ 5
```

Sequence (a): 1♡ - 1NT, NB. Best defence could hold this to 6 tricks but it would be difficult for West to know that he should put his ♣A on the first round and, in practice, 1NT is likely to make.

Sequence (b): 1♡ - 1NT, 2◇ - NB. Not a riotous success. The defence makes the automatic trump lead (p. 148–9) and declarer is restricted to 6 tricks.

Sequence (c): 1♡ - 1NT, 2◇ - 2♡. North should be wary of showing false preference here. The South hand could be 4-4-4-1, as it is. The bad break makes it three off.

Sequence (d): 1♡ - 1NT, 2◇ - 3♣. Declarer loses only one club trick and three diamonds so this seems the best contract. What is the reason for this? The key is that the club suit is reasonably solid, and the weak hand is playing the contract, the only way of gaining entries to North.

So, should we be proud of sequence (d)? No, not exactly. It is rather fortunate that North has such a solid suit to retreat to. If he were missing just one of his club honours he would have been unable to draw the trumps and the contract would have become very difficult to play. Sequence (a) is the one that will pay off on most hands. After all, North can't have a four-card major suit (or he would have supported hearts or bid 1♠), nor has he enough diamonds to support your suit, so he is likely to have club length. 1NT will give you the best chance of a positive score in the majority of cases.

♠ 5
♡ A K Q 4 3 2
◇ A 9 3
♣ 7 6 5

You are West, with both sides vulnerable. You open 1♡ and your partner responds 1♠. What is your rebid?

You have a powerful hand, with 13 high card points, two distributional points and a great heart suit. You can count the hand for about 7 playing tricks. If your partner had responded 2♣ or 2◇, or even 1NT you would have been happy to make a jump rebid of 3♡, but unfortunately he has bid 1♠, and that should cause you to think. If much of partner's strength is in spades, you are likely to be left with a lot of losers in the minor suits, and if you rebid 3♡ you may be too high. If, on the other hand, partner can help you in the diamond suit and has a shortage in clubs, then 4♡ may be making. So you will have to take a view.

Fits and Misfits

The full deal:

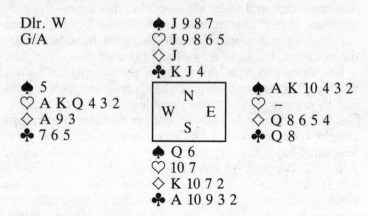

Dlr. W
G/A

♠ J 9 8 7
♡ J 9 8 6 5
♢ J
♣ K J 4

♠ 5
♡ A K Q 4 3 2
♢ A 9 3
♣ 7 6 5

♠ A K 10 4 3 2
♡ –
♢ Q 8 6 5 4
♣ Q 8

♠ Q 6
♡ 10 7
♢ K 10 7 2
♣ A 10 9 3 2

In practice the bidding started 1♡-1♠, 3♡ and East went straight to 4♠, completely ignoring the misfitting features of the hand. Worse was to come. West now went to 5♡, bidding his values the third time over, North doubled and East rescued into 5♠, also doubled and three down.

Of course, West has an awkward rebid. If he downgrades the hand and rebids only 2♡ he will miss a game if East has, for example, ♠ A-x-x-x-x, ♡ x-x, ♢ Q-J-10-x, ♣ x-x, or many other limited hands. No one likes to miss a game, so most West players would rebid 3♡, hoping that partner had at least a semi-fit for their suit. It is reasonable to take some risk in the bidding if there is the chance of a game or slam but important to limit the damage when the misfitting features are confirmed.

♠ A K J 9 2
♡ A 3
♢ Q 10 7
♣ 9 6 5

You are East, dealer, with both sides vulnerable. You open 1♠ and your partner responds 1NT. You decide (probably unwisely, see p. 63) to bid 2♠, and he bids 3♣. What do you do now?

Ask yourself what possible reason partner can have for insisting on his minor suit. It can't be a try for game because he has already limited his hand with his response of 1NT. He must hate your spades like poison and be desperate to play in his long suit. This is *not* a hand for going on. Although you fit his clubs quite well, he has already announced weakness, and you should take this sequence as a definite command to pass.

The full deal:

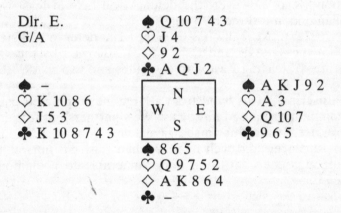

```
        Dlr. E.           ♠ Q 10 7 4 3
        G/A               ♡ J 4
                          ◇ 9 2
                          ♣ A Q J 2
     ♠ -                                  ♠ A K J 9 2
     ♡ K 10 8 6          N               ♡ A 3
     ◇ J 5 3         W         E         ◇ Q 10 7
     ♣ K 10 8 7 4 3        S             ♣ 9 6 5
                          ♠ 8 6 5
                          ♡ Q 9 7 5 2
                          ◇ A K 8 6 4
                          ♣ -
```

West has the sort of hand that is seldom discussed in books but occurs sometimes at the table, where one *has* to find an answer. East opens 1♠ and West might consider a pass but the problem is that 1♠ may be the only unplayable contract, with a safe part-score or even a game possible in some other suit. However, to respond 2♣ would greatly overstate the value of the hand and may well drive partner back into spades. West is forced, therefore, to respond 1NT, although normally one needs at least a semi-fit in partner's suit to make the play of a no-trump contract comfortable. If East passes 1NT, this is unlikely, on most hands, to be worse than 1♠; if he rebids in a red suit West will be delighted and if East rebids his spades, West can simply sign off in 3♣ (the actual sequence).

West may be lucky in 3♣ because North has an awkward lead. He will not wish to lead a club into the West hand or a spade, as it may help to set up dummy's suit. He will have to guess between hearts and diamonds. If he chooses a heart, West will go up with dummy's ace, then play the ♠ A-K, discarding two diamonds. Now a heart back to the ♡K and a low heart towards dummy will assure West of the contract. If North finds the diamond lead, however, the defence will take at least two diamond and three club tricks.

In 2♠ East really has no hope. The defence will start with the ♢ A-K and ♢4 (ruffed), followed by the ♣2 (ruffed), leaving East with two clubs and two spades still to lose.

Postscript: This hand from a large match-pointed pairs competition caused most East-West partnerships to come to grief. Three clubs made gave a very good score. Some West players did well in 1NT when East did not rebid, although the contract is very vulnerable to a diamond lead.

♠ K Q 7 6 3	You are dealer, West, with neither
♡ K 8 3	side vulnerable. You open 1♠, your
♢ Q	partner responds 1NT and you rebid
♣ A Q 8 5	2♣. Partner now bids 2♢. What do you do?

For heaven's sake, heed the gipsy's warning and pass. Partner has told you he is limited with his 1NT response, and he may have had to scrape up the bid on all sorts of holdings. He knows what you have and if he chooses to ignore your spades and clubs and to run out into diamonds, who are you to argue?

The full deal:

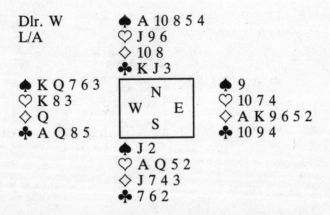

Dlr. W
L/A

♠ A 10 8 5 4
♡ J 9 6
◇ 10 8
♣ K J 3

♠ K Q 7 6 3
♡ K 8 3
◇ Q
♣ A Q 8 5

♠ 9
♡ 10 7 4
◇ A K 9 6 5 2
♣ 10 9 4

♠ J 2
♡ A Q 5 2
◇ J 7 4 3
♣ 7 6 2

Too many players look at the sixteen points in the West hand and go on to 2NT. This has no chance at all as the diamond suit can't be established because of lack of entries to dummy. Poor East has then to go back to 3◇, which has little chance.

♠ A K 9 3 2
♡ Q 2
◇ K J 7
♣ 10 8 7

You are West, dealer, with neither side vulnerable. You open 1♠ and your partner responds 1NT. What is your rebid?

Although your spades are rebiddable, it is better to pass. If your partner has a semi-fit for spades the play of 1NT should be straightforward. If he hates your spades he will not thank you for insisting on your suit.

The full deal:

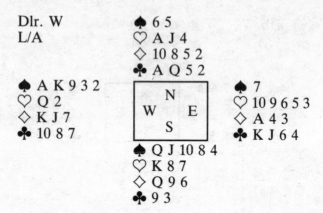

```
Dlr. W          ♠ 6 5
L/A             ♡ A J 4
                ◇ 10 8 5 2
                ♣ A Q 5 2
♠ A K 9 3 2                      ♠ 7
♡ Q 2           N               ♡ 10 9 6 5 3
◇ K J 7      W     E             ◇ A 4 3
♣ 10 8 7        S               ♣ K J 6 4
                ♠ Q J 10 8 4
                ♡ K 8 7
                ◇ Q 9 6
                ♣ 9 3
```

With the misfit in spades, East back-pedalled with a 1NT response, a reasonable spot when West has the sense to pass.

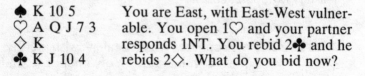

♠ K 10 5   You are East, with East-West vulner-
♡ A Q J 7 3   able. You open 1♡ and your partner
◇ K   responds 1NT. You rebid 2♣ and he
♣ K J 10 4   rebids 2◇. What do you bid now?

This is another hand where you should heed the warning signs. You have described your hand shape accurately as at least five hearts and four clubs. Partner has rejected both your suits and insisted on diamonds. Surely he must have six. Also he cannot be strong, for his first response was 1NT, so there is no hope of anything more than a part-score. At least you have the king of his suit so you can just about stand diamonds, but the hand is beginning to look like a nasty misfit and it will not pay you to be ambitious.

The bidding:

	West	East
		1♡
	1NT	2♣
	2♢	NB

The full deal:

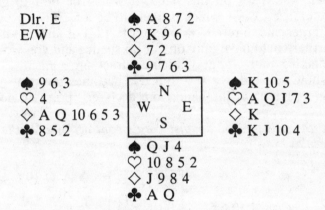

Dlr. E
E/W

♠ A 8 7 2
♡ K 9 6
♢ 7 2
♣ 9 7 6 3

♠ 9 6 3
♡ 4
♢ A Q 10 6 5 3
♣ 8 5 2

♠ K 10 5
♡ A Q J 7 3
♢ K
♣ K J 10 4

♠ Q J 4
♡ 10 8 5 2
♢ J 9 8 4
♣ A Q

Even though West lost two spades, a diamond and two clubs, he just made his contract. This proved to be an excellent result. Several Easts had tried 2NT and others had gone back to 2♡, but these contracts seldom made because, with the entry problems that always occur on misfitting hands, dummy's diamonds were wasted. As we saw before, on an earlier hand, a response of 1NT followed by a retreat to a minor suit should be treated as a command to pass. This hand is another classic illustration of the efficiency of using a 1NT response as a prelude to a sign-off.

♠ A Q 10 6 4
♡ 10 3
♢ 9 2
♣ J 8 6 4

You are East, with neither side vulnerable. Your partner, West, opens 1♡, you respond 1♠ and he rebids 2♢. What do you bid now?

Fits and Misfits

As explained on p. 24, it is the modern style to open 1NT on hands with two 4-card suits, if in the 12-14 point range, or to open one of a suit and rebid no-trumps if stronger. When two suits are bid these days it usually shows a hand shape of 5-4 or better (or a hand with three four-card suits). Partner cannot be 4-4-4-1 or he would have raised your spades so, on this hand, it would be best to give preference to 2♡, which is likely to be a 5-2 fit. It would be gruesome to rebid 2♠ on your hand. For all you know partner could have only one or no spades and you would be taking yourself out of a fair contract into a misfit. Let's assume you bid 2♡ and that this becomes the contract, and now look at the hand from declarer's point of view:

North leads the ♠2 against West's contract of 2♡. Plan the play.

♠ 3		♠ A Q 10 6 4
♡ A J 9 4 2		♡ 10 3
◇ K J 10 6 5		◇ 9 2
♣ K 3		♣ J 8 6 4

Planning and play: You have to go up with the ♠A but this is your only entry to dummy, so you must decide immediately whether to run the ♡10 from dummy or the ◇9, intending to finesse against South in either case. It is better to try running the ◇9. If South has the ◇Q you may be able to get away with the loss of only one trick in the suit. You can't enter dummy again to take another finesse. In any case the only situation in which a heart finesse would help is if South held both ♡K and ♡Q, and this is against the odds.

74

The full deal:

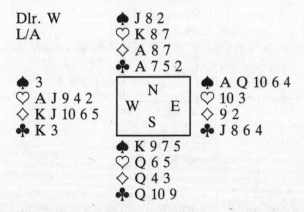

Dlr. W   ♠ J 8 2
L/A   ♡ K 8 7
          ◇ A 8 7
          ♣ A 7 5 2

♠ 3   ♠ A Q 10 6 4
♡ A J 9 4 2   ♡ 10 3
◇ K J 10 6 5   ◇ 9 2
♣ K 3   ♣ J 8 6 4

          ♠ K 9 7 5
          ♡ Q 6 5
          ◇ Q 4 3
          ♣ Q 10 9

If South covers the ◇9, West will play the ◇K to force out the ◇A. If South ducks the ◇9 and North wins with the ◇A, declarer can later play ◇K and ◇5, ruffed in dummy, to establish the suit. With four diamond tricks, three hearts and a spade, West should bring home his contract.

So far, in this chapter, we have seen a number of misfitting hands on which the partnership should stay low, to avoid poor results. However, not all hands that appear as nasty misfits should be played in unambitious contracts. Two examples follow:

Dlr. S   ♠ J
E/W   ♡ A K 8 7 5 3 2
           ♢ –
           ♣ A J 7 6 5

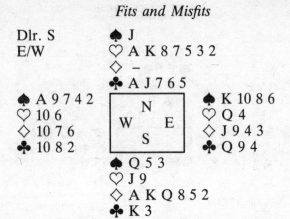

♠ A 9 7 4 2   ♠ K 10 8 6
♡ 10 6   ♡ Q 4
♢ 10 7 6   ♢ J 9 4 3
♣ 10 8 2   ♣ Q 9 4

         ♠ Q 5 3
         ♡ J 9
         ♢ A K Q 8 5 2
         ♣ K 3

South opened 1♢ and rebid 2♢ over his partner's response of 1♡. North lost ambition and went straight to 4♡. Even though East made the best lead, the ♠6, North had 12 tricks on top when the ♡Q fell on the second round of trumps.

If North had forced with a response of 2♡, and then rebid his hearts, North-South *might* have bid the slam. However, it is likely that North would back-pedal in view of his apparent misfit in diamonds and the slam would be hard to bid. Twelve tricks are made because the ♡Q drops (a 52% chance). The features that made the slam possible are the seven-card heart suit, the presence of five solid tricks in the side suits and nine first or second round controls in the partnership hands. Thus, the slam makes despite the misfitting features.

A similar hand from a Swiss Pairs event is shown overleaf:

Dlr. S
E/W

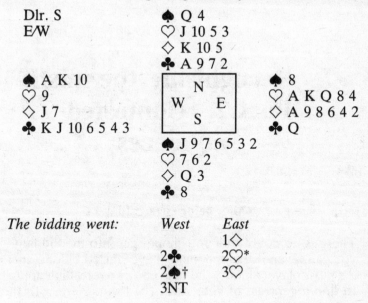

	♠ Q 4	
	♡ J 10 5 3	
	◇ K 10 5	
	♣ A 9 7 2	
♠ A K 10		♠ 8
♡ 9		♡ A K Q 8 4
◇ J 7		◇ A 9 8 6 4 2
♣ K J 10 6 5 4 3		♣ Q
	♠ J 9 7 6 5 3 2	
	♡ 7 6 2	
	◇ Q 3	
	♣ 8	

The bidding went:

West	East
	1◇
2♣	2♡*
2♠†	3♡
3NT	

* Forcing 'reverse'
† Fourth suit forcing

Seeing the hand as something of a misfit, East-West settled quietly in 3NT. 6♣, however, will make, even on a diamond lead because there are immediate discards on the hearts. Is this a sound contract or are we just being 'results merchants'?

The features to note are (a) West has a seven-card suit, (b) East has the queen of his partner's suit (sheer gold) and (c) the partnership has six solid tricks in the side suits. So perhaps this, too, is an exceptional hand.

So, by being cautious on the apparent misfits you may occasionally miss the boat. However, you will almost certainly gain in the long run by avoiding a considerable number of disagreeable contracts.

7 Recognising the misfit
Part 2   Contested Sequences

Think before overcalling

There is no doubt that you should get into the bidding if
you can, even if the opponents have started bidding first.
As most players know, the reasons for overcalling are (a)
to find a contract of your own, (b) to interfere with the
opponents' bidding sequence, (c) to suggest a sacrifice
contract if the opponents appear to have found a good
fit, (d) to give partner information on which he may be
able to base a penalty double if the opponents get too
high, (e) to deflect the opponents from a no-trump contract that they might otherwise make, if you do not intervene, and (f) to suggest a good lead if your side defends.

However, you need to consider the circumstances, and
the vulnerability, before you enter the auction.

♠ 8 3 2	If your right-hand opponent opens
♡ K Q J 4 3	1♠ it might be reasonable to come in
◇ A J	with 2♡ (not vulnerable) because of
♣ Q 10 9	all the reasons given above.

Of course, you *might* get doubled, but your left-hand
opponent needs a very precise type of hand (p. 114–6) to
do this, and he doesn't exactly know his partner's shape

and strength, so it is difficult for him to judge. If the opening bid is 1NT, there is much greater danger in intervening. Now responder does know his partner's strength within very close limits and is guaranteed at least two hearts in opener's hand, so he will be in a good position to judge the situation and to double you, if that looks best.

Thus, in all overcalling situations, one has to balance the potential risks against the potential gains. Ask yourself the two questions, 'What will happen if I bid? What will happen if I pass?' In the example given on p. 78, if the opponents stay in spades, your hearts may be trumped, so you may have very few defensive tricks, whilst, if you bid, you are not all that likely to be doubled. In contrast, if the opponents play in no-trumps you have a good lead ($\heartsuit$K) and entries, so you may be able to put up a very effective defence. Also, any action by you is *more* likely to be punished, if the cards sit badly, so an overcall is less attractive over 1NT than over 1♠.

However, if we strengthened your suit to $\heartsuit$ K-Q-J-10-4-3, by swopping a low spade for the $\heartsuit$10, you could confidently bid 2$\heartsuit$ over 1♠ or 1NT, because your chances of the opponents having a profitable double of a heart contract are much reduced. You may think that it is not worth disturbing 1NT as you are likely to defeat it on a heart lead, but this often turns out to be a false hope because responder may bid spades, and now you will have lost your chance to compete in hearts or to guide your partner's opening lead.

If you are borderline for an overcall, look out for any clues as to how well the hands fit, to help you to reach a decision. For example, length in the opponents' suits is often a bad feature, particularly length in a suit that your left-hand opponent has called; any high cards you have in that suit will be badly placed and your attempt to ruff the suit in your partner's hand may result in an over-ruff. Although not as bad, length in the suit that your right-hand opponent has called is not encouraging. Your high cards in that suit will be well placed now but the indication is that the partnership hands are not really fitting. However, if you have the top cards in the opponent's suit, you need not be too worried; it is *losers* in their suit that you are keen to avoid.

Action when partner has overcalled

Your first thought should be whether you can raise partner's suit. Three-card support is ample, as he will have at least a five-card suit. However, you must be careful not to raise him too high, for he will not be strong in outside values, particularly if his overcall was made at the one-level, and your side is not vulnerable.

But what happens if you hate his suit and want to bid your own suit? Players have different views on the meaning of 2♡ in a sequence such as this:

West	North	East	South
1♠	2♢	NB	2♡

Some like to play it as a forcing bid, others as a constructive bid (showing some tolerance at least for overcaller's suit), whilst a third school of thought likes to play it as a complete sign-off, saying 'the contract has to be played in *my* suit, partner'. We are in favour of choosing one of the first two styles. The third style is too unilateral for our taste; how can South *know* that his suit will be better than his partner's? The hand has every appearance of being a misfit, so it is best to give up quietly. North has not yet been doubled, so South has no need to panic, and if he passes quietly, West may let him off the hook by bidding again. In other words *don't 'rescue' partner until you have to*. One clear situation where an immediate rescue is in order is when one opponent has doubled your partner for take-out, and the other opponent has converted it into a penalty double by passing. For example:

West	North	East	South
1♣	NB	NB	Dbl
NB	NB	?	

West opened 1♣ in all innocence and passed when South doubled for take-out, expecting North to bid. However, North has all the spades sitting over him, and so passed for penalties. Now East must rescue his partner because another pass will close the auction and West will be left in the trap.

The hand shown below illustrates the point:

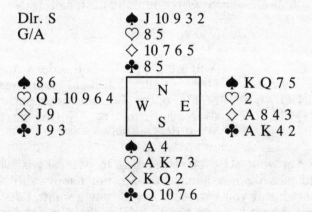

```
Dlr. S        ♠ J 10 9 3 2
G/A           ♡ 8 5
              ◇ 10 7 6 5
              ♣ 8 5

♠ 8 6                      ♠ K Q 7 5
♡ Q J 10 9 6 4            ♡ 2
◇ J 9          W   E       ◇ A 8 4 3
♣ J 9 3                    ♣ A K 4 2

              ♠ A 4
              ♡ A K 7 3
              ◇ K Q 2
              ♣ Q 10 7 6
```

South opens 1♡, followed by two passes. Now East doubles 1♡ protectively, South passes and West passes. North must rescue, against reasonable opponents. He will probably bid 1♠, and North-South will have found a good spot.

A variation of this situation occurs in the following example:

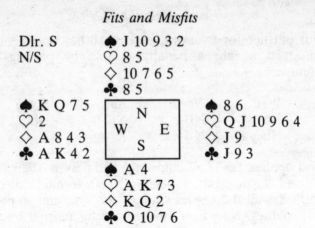

Dlr. S   ♠ J 10 9 3 2
N/S   ♡ 8 5
         ◇ 10 7 6 5
         ♣ 8 5

♠ K Q 7 5   ♠ 8 6
♡ 2   ♡ Q J 10 9 6 4
◇ A 8 4 3   ◇ J 9
♣ A K 4 2   ♣ J 9 3

         ♠ A 4
         ♡ A K 7 3
         ◇ K Q 2
         ♣ Q 10 7 6

South opens 1♡, West doubles for take-out, North passes, and East passes for penalties. Now South must rescue himself. An SOS redouble is best, letting North choose the suit.

♠ 6   You are East, with both sides vulner-
♡ 10 9 5 2   able. Your left-hand opponent,
◇ K Q 7 6 5   South, opens 1♣ and your partner
♣ Q 7 5   overcalls with 1♠. North passes.
                  What do you bid?

Whatever your style of responding to overcalls is, you should pass on this hand. You are not happy with the contract but if you wriggle you will only get into deeper trouble. There is no reason to believe that the hand will play better in one of your suits than in partner's spades (he must have at least a five-card suit for an overcall) and any action from you will simply force him to a higher level.

But what if North doubles for penalties? You would still pass. All the arguments given above still apply. You should not 'rescue' partner in this type of situation as nothing would be more maddening for him to be taken out of a contract that may be making into one of your suits that will probably go down.

So, let's assume that 1♠ is passed out and that North leads ♣10 (his partner's suit). Now let's look at the play from West's point of view, as shown below.

North leads the ♣10 against West's contract of 1♠. Plan the play.

```
♠ A Q J 10 4          ┌─────────┐          ♠ 6
♡ K 8 7               │    N    │          ♡ 10 9 5 2
♢ 10 8              W │         │ E        ♢ K Q 7 6 5
♣ A 8 2               │    S    │          ♣ Q 7 5
                      └─────────┘
```

Planning and play: It looks as if the ♣K-J lie over the ♣Q and that you will only make one club trick. You are short of entries to dummy and will have to make the most of your single sure entry to that hand. South may be presumed to hold most of the high cards but should you finesse him for the ♠K or ♡A? It is far better to finesse the heart when you are in dummy; the spade finesse may succeed but you can't repeat it and South will still make his ♠K unless he started with precisely ♠K-x, very much against the odds. If you try the heart finesse however, and it succeeds, that is one trick 'in the bag' and you will not be forced to lead away from your ♡ K-x-x later. So, win with the ♣A and play ♠A and ♠Q from your hand, giving up a trump trick, and later use the diamond entry in dummy to finesse the heart. The principle is similar to that on pp. 74–5.

```
♠ J 2          You are East, with both sides vulner-
♡ 2            able. Your   left-hand   opponent,
♢ Q 10 5 3     South, opens 1♢, your partner over-
♣ Q J 9 6 4 3  calls 1♡ and North doubles. What do
               you do?
```

Fits and Misfits

The situation seems, at first sight, to be similar to that on the last hand; your partner has made a one-level over-call in a suit in which you have only a singleton, and he has been doubled for penalties. On the last hand you were advised to leave him to it. Should you do the same now?

No, this time we advise you to run to 2♣. There are two important differences from the last hand. Then you had a stronger hand, with the ◇ K-Q providing a trick. This also gave an entry into dummy, and the opportunity to lead towards declarer's hand for a finesse. In contrast, if West is left to play in 1♡ doubled on this deal, it is very unlikely that he will make a single trick in your hand and he will be forced to lead *away* from all his high cards. More important still, this time you have a *six-card suit* with some reasonable intermediates. Played in clubs you may make an extra three or four tricks, so it's well worth going up one level.

The full deal:

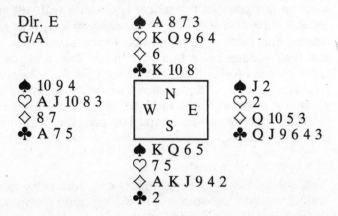

```
        Dlr. E        ♠ A 8 7 3
        G/A           ♡ K Q 9 6 4
                      ◇ 6
                      ♣ K 10 8
  ♠ 10 9 4                            ♠ J 2
  ♡ A J 10 8 3      N                ♡ 2
  ◇ 8 7         W        E           ◇ Q 10 5 3
  ♣ A 7 5              S             ♣ Q J 9 6 4 3
                      ♠ K Q 6 5
                      ♡ 7 5
                      ◇ A K J 9 4 2
                      ♣ 2
```

In a recent teams match the East player in one room ran to 2♣ and escaped for one off doubled. In the other room, East passed the double of 1♡, and South and West also passed.

North led his singleton diamond, South won with the ◇J and switched to the ♣2. West should have put up his ♣A and played ♡A and another heart to draw South's trumps, but he didn't. So North won with the ♣K and gave his partner a ruff. South returned a spade and North gave him another ruff. Declarer emerged with only three tricks and an 1100 penalty. Even if declarer plays his best it is difficult to see how he could come to more than four tricks.

The East player who rescued his partner from 1♡ doubled was guided by four considerations. (1) The double of 1♡ told him that the trumps were stacked against his partner. (2) He had only a singleton in his partner's suit. (3) In a heart contract there was no trick (and no entry) in the East hand. (4) The East hand contained a *six*-card suit that should provide a reasonable resting place. When put all together, they became an irresistible argument for a rescue into 2♣.

Postscript: The North-South side have a spade contract of course, but they are unlikely to make a game in spades against accurate defence. The defence is discussed in more detail later in the book (p. 144) 3 NT is makeable, but who will bid it?

♠ 3
♡ J 10 4 3
◇ K 9 8 4 3 2
♣ Q 8

You are East, with both sides vulnerable. Your partner, West, opens 1♠ and North doubles. What do you bid?

You should pass. In days gone by a bid from you now would indicate an escape into a long weak suit and on this hand you may well wish that you could play it this way. The modern style, however, is to ignore the double and bid naturally. A bid of 2◇, therefore, would show

at least eight points and be a forward-going, encouraging
move. With a misfit for spades and the ♣ Q-8 not worth
two points, forward would be the wrong direction.

You pass, South passes and West bids 2♣, doubled by
North. So the bidding has been:

West	North	East	South
1♠	Dbl	NB	NB
2♣	Dbl	?	

What should you do now?

Let's review what the bidding has told us. West opened
1♠ and North doubled for take-out, showing a shortage
of spades but support for the other three suits. When you
passed, South also passed, so he must have a massive
spade holding and expects to defeat 1♠ doubled. Your
partner, West, then escaped to 2♣. North's second
double must be for penalties because his take-out double
indicated that he held good clubs and he can't be asking
South for his suit as he knows that South holds spades.
Now is the time to rescue from what is likely to be only
a 4-2 trump fit. You bid 2◇, and this is passed round to
North, who doubles.

The full deal:

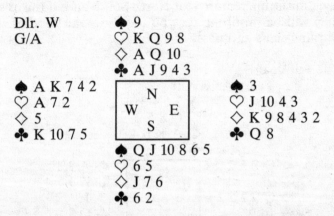

Dlr. W
G/A

	♠ 9	
	♡ K Q 9 8	
	◇ A Q 10	
	♣ A J 9 4 3	

♠ A K 7 4 2   ♠ 3
♡ A 7 2   ♡ J 10 4 3
◇ 5   ◇ K 9 8 4 3 2
♣ K 10 7 5   ♣ Q 8

	♠ Q J 10 8 6 5	
	♡ 6 5	
	◇ J 7 6	
	♣ 6 2	

Postscript: Although the 3-3 diamond split is lucky, it's interesting to note how East-West avoided a very large penalty. East hung back on the misfit at first. Only when West had described his hand by bidding two black suits, and been doubled in both, did East introduce his diamonds. We know, from p. 61, that a player will be most reluctant to insist on his own suit when his partner has shown two suits, so West should recognise the hopelessness of a black suit contract and accept East's decision, despite his singleton diamond.

♠ A J 10   You are East, with East-West vulner-
♡ K J 7 4 3   able. Your left hand opponent,
◇ J   South, opens 1♣ and North responds
♣ Q J 8 6   1◇. Do you intervene?

The heart suit might be better but you have 13 high-card points. Normally you might overcall in this situation, but there are two indications against it. Firstly, you are vulnerable, and to go down could be costly. Second, there is a cloud on the horizon in the shape of your four clubs, sitting under South's holding. It looks as if the hands have misfitting features for North-South and, if this is so, they will be misfitting for you too. So, take heed of the warning signs and pass.

The full deal:

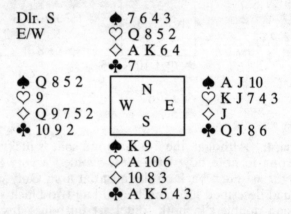

Dlr. S
E/W

North: ♠ 7 6 4 3 ♡ Q 8 5 2 ◇ A K 6 4 ♣ 7

West: ♠ Q 8 5 2 ♡ 9 ◇ Q 9 7 5 2 ♣ 10 9 2

East: ♠ A J 10 ♡ K J 7 4 3 ◇ J ♣ Q J 8 6

South: ♠ K 9 ♡ A 10 6 ◇ 10 8 3 ♣ A K 5 4 3

If South opens 1♣, North responds 1◇ and East intervenes with 1♡, South's best action is to pass. He has nothing to be ashamed of but no particular message to impart, so he leaves the bidding to go round to his partner. With a singleton in clubs and four cards in East's suit, North will also pass and East will have no hope in his 1♡ contract. Remember you don't *have* to bid just because you've got 13 points.

If East chooses to pass, North-South may not do so well. South may rebid 2♣ or, if his methods allow, 1NT. Even if he makes his contract he will score less than by defeating a vulnerable 1♡. There are lessons in the bidding, for both sides.

♠ K 10 7 6 5 3   You are West, with neither side
♡ K   vulnerable. Your left hand opponent,
♢ 9 7 6 4 2   North, opens 1♡. Your partner over-
♣ 6   calls with 2♣ and South passes. What
                 do you bid?

It's unfortunate that partner chose clubs and the hand
looks like a nasty misfit. Obviously you have no intention
of 'rescuing' because, for all you know, partner's clubs
are much better than either of your suits. Anyway, he has
not been doubled yet and there's no point in panicking. If
you pass now, North may let you off the hook by repeating his hearts or bidding another suit.

So you pass, and North reopens the bidding with a
double. East and South both pass, and it's up to you
again.

The bidding so far: West   North   East   South
                                 1♡   2♣   NB
                         NB   Dbl   NB   NB
                         ?

Now the position has changed completely. North's
reopening double is for take-out, not for penalties. We
shall see other examples of this bid in Chapter 8. South
is expected to bid, but has passed, thus converting his
partner's take-out double into a penalty double. So,
although he is not strong, South has a good club holding
sitting over your partner. The time has come to take
evasive action, and your rescue into 2♠ shouldn't be
misinterpreted. The full deal is shown overleaf:

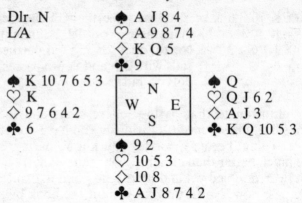

Dlr. N
L/A

♠ A J 8 4
♡ A 9 8 7 4
◇ K Q 5
♣ 9

♠ K 10 7 6 5 3
♡ K
◇ 9 7 6 4 2
♣ 6

♠ Q
♡ Q J 6 2
◇ A J 3
♣ K Q 10 5 3

♠ 9 2
♡ 10 5 3
◇ 10 8
♣ A J 8 7 4 2

North may double 2♠, of course, and is likely to defeat it by one or two tricks. Still, that's not too disastrous for East-West. 2♣ doubled would have been worse, for there is no entry at all to the West hand and declarer would probably emerge with only two heart tricks, one diamond and at most two clubs, giving a penalty of 500 points.

Postscript: South was correct to pass the 2♣ overcall at first. He has too much in his partner's suit and too little defensive strength for an immediate penalty double. However, North's reopening double, followed by South's penalty pass, created a potentially disastrous situation for East-West, so West was forced to take action.

East put his side in danger by overcalling 2♣. He ignored the cloud on the horizon . . . he has four hearts, his opponent's suit, so there is just the smell of a misfit in the air.

♠ 8 6 5 3 2
♡ 4
◇ Q 9 8 4
♣ 9 8 2

You are North, with neither side vulnerable. Your partner, South, opens 1♡ and West passes. What do you bid?

Obviously, with a misfit and only two points you pass.

You can see the storm clouds gathering. East doubles for take-out, South and West both pass. So the bidding has been:

South	West	North	East
1♡	NB	NB	Dbl
NB	NB	?	

Again we have the classic situation where you *should* rescue partner. East has doubled for take-out and West has converted to a penalty double by passing, so you should run. West is likely to be sitting over your partner's hearts and you can hardly be in a worse spot than 1♡ doubled. You must bid 1♠. You are not showing any strength; you have already passed his opening bid. You are simply trying to save him from a fate worse than death.

The full deal:

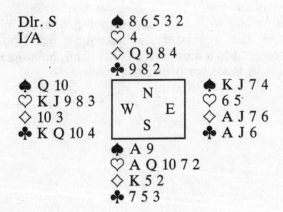

```
Dlr. S          ♠ 8 6 5 3 2
L/A             ♡ 4
                ◇ Q 9 8 4
                ♣ 9 8 2
♠ Q 10                          ♠ K J 7 4
♡ K J 9 8 3        N            ♡ 6 5
◇ 10 3          W     E         ◇ A J 7 6
♣ K Q 10 4         S            ♣ A J 6
                ♠ A 9
                ♡ A Q 10 7 2
                ◇ K 5 2
                ♣ 7 5 3
```

As can be seen 1♠ is only slightly better, and East is likely to double this too. However, there are four certain tricks as against three certain tricks in 1♡ doubled. On this hand, this is about as good as North-South are likely to do against keen opposition.

♠ 8 5 4	You are South, with North-South
♡ 3	vulnerable. Your partner opens 1♡
◇ K 8 7 5 4 3	and the next player passes. What do
♣ Q 9 7	you bid?

You dislike the hearts intensely and would like to play in your suit but there's nothing you can do at present. A one-level contract in hearts can't be too bad and, if West takes some action, you may be let off the hook.

You pass and West doubles for take-out. North and East both pass. So the bidding has gone:

The bidding:	North	East	South	West
	1♡	NB	NB	Dbl
	NB	NB	?	

What do you bid now?

Again we are in the familiar situation where a rescue is more or less mandatory, so you must bid 2◇, and unless partner has a most exceptional hand, he must pass. The full deal is shown overleaf:

Dlr. N
N/S

♠ 6 2
♡ K J 8 4 2
♢ A 2
♣ A 10 4 3

♠ A K 9 7
♡ A 6
♢ Q J 6
♣ J 8 6 2

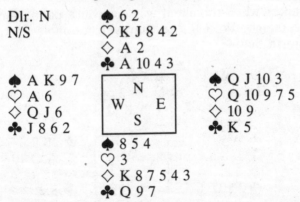

♠ Q J 10 3
♡ Q 10 9 7 5
♢ 10 9
♣ K 5

♠ 8 5 4
♡ 3
♢ K 8 7 5 4 3
♣ Q 9 7

North would have been at least two down in 1♡ doubled as he would have had to lose two spade tricks, and possibly four hearts, in addition to two clubs. In two diamonds, South may lose only three spade tricks, one heart, one diamond and one club and he may not even be doubled. Over 2♢, passed by West and North, East may decide that it is more profitable to bid 2♠ for a safe part score.

♠ 5 4
♡ 7 4 2
♢ A K Q 9 8 3
♣ K 4

You are North, with neither side vulnerable. Your right hand opponent opens 1NT. What do you bid?

If the hand is played in your long suit you should make six diamond tricks, and there is a 50-50 chance of a trick in clubs. With so many playing tricks you can afford to overcall at the two level and you would do so even if vulnerable. Over your 2♢, the next two hands pass and West doubles. What do you make of that?

Well, the double is impossible, of course. Once West has opened with a weak 1NT he has shown his full hand and he must leave all further action to his partner. Never-

Fits and Misfits

theless when this hand was dealt in a pairs event a few years ago, West *did* reopen with a double on the hand shown below:

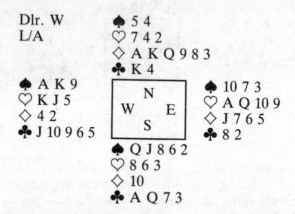

Dlr. W
L/A

North: ♠ 5 4 ♡ 7 4 2 ◇ A K Q 9 8 3 ♣ K 4

West: ♠ A K 9 ♡ K J 5 ◇ 4 2 ♣ J 10 9 6 5

East: ♠ 10 7 3 ♡ A Q 10 9 ◇ J 7 6 5 ♣ 8 2

South: ♠ Q J 8 6 2 ♡ 8 6 3 ◇ 10 ♣ A Q 7 3

North passed the double, East took out into 2♡, South and West passed and North went to 3◇, doubled by East.

So the bidding had been:

The bidding:	West	North	East	South
	1NT	2◇	NB	NB
	Dbl	NB	2♡	NB
	NB	3◇	Dbl	

This contract went two down for an appalling result for North-South, so what exactly went wrong and who was to blame?

The first round of bidding, 1NT-2◇-NB-NB was quite sound but West's double (presumably for take-out) was a try-on. East was forced to bid 2♡ but now both South and North went wrong. With a singleton in his partner's suit and 9 points South could have doubled 2♡. As it was he passed and North blundered on to 3◇.

Postscript: Neither 2♡ by East nor 3◇ by North should make on these misfitting hands. North and South failed to handle the unfamiliar auction, both of them making mistakes. South missed the chance of a double that would have warned his partner of the situation and, although quite strong, North bid his values twice.

♠ A J 7 6 5   You are North, vulnerable, and you
♡ A K 7 3 2   open 1♠. East doubles, South passes
♢ 2   and West bids 2♢. You bid 2♡, East
♣ 6 4   doubles again and there are two
                 passes back to you.

So the bidding has gone:

West	North	East	South
	1♠	Dbl	NB
2♢	2♡	Dbl	NB
NB	?		

What do you bid now?

In practice, North retreated to 2♠ and this was *not* a success. The full deal is shown below:

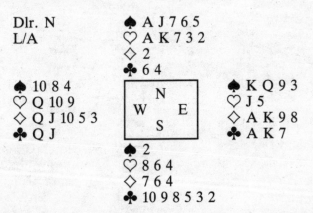

Dlr. N
L/A

♠ A J 7 6 5
♡ A K 7 3 2
♢ 2
♣ 6 4

♠ 10 8 4   ♠ K Q 9 3
♡ Q 10 9   ♡ J 5
♢ Q J 10 5 3   ♢ A K 9 8
♣ Q J   ♣ A K 7

♠ 2
♡ 8 6 4
♢ 7 6 4
♣ 10 9 8 5 3 2

A forcing defence (diamond lead and continuation) resulted in the contract being three down.

North should have remembered that the double can show a variety of hands, not simply a take-out double of 1♠ (see p. 34–6). In fact East had the balanced type of hand that is too strong for an overcall of 1NT. The point that North missed was that his partner had chosen hearts when he passed East's second double, and North was wrong to go back to his first suit.

Postscript: If 2♡ doubled is left to play, the best defence is to lead trumps, which gets 2♡ one off.

8   Reopening the Bidding

Sometimes, to find a fit for his side, a player has to reopen the bidding to prevent it from dying. Most players are familiar with the principle of reopening the bidding in the *protective position* which, in its simplest form, occurs after a sequence such as the following:

Sequence (a)

West	North	East	South
1◇	NB	NB	?

South is in the protective position. He can reason that, since West has opened with only a one-level bid, and East has not even the strength to reply, then North must be marked with some points, so it's safe to reopen the bidding on quite modest values. The subject of protective bidding is discussed in all the bidding text books, so we won't go into it in detail here. The simple example given above is only one of a number of reopening situations in which a player makes a bid (or double) after passes by the two preceding players. In all these cases, there is an indication, from the bidding, that the reopening side has the values to compete.

Sequence (b)   Responder makes a limit raise of opener's suit, and opener passes. Thus:

West	North	East	South
1◇	NB	2◇	NB
NB	?		

As East and West have both limited their hands, North could consider reopening the bidding on a modest hand with a reasonable suit.

Sequence (c) Opener raises responder's suit, and responder passes. Thus:

West	North	East	South
1♣	NB	1♡	NB
2♡	NB	NB	?

East-West have again found a suit fit, but are stopping in a low-level contract. The implication is that North-South have a suit fit too, and enough strength to make a part-score.

Sequence (d) Responder has given preference to opener's first suit, and opener has passed. Thus:

West	North	East	South
1♡	NB	1NT	NB
2♣	NB	2♡	NB
NB	?		

North can consider coming in. He could only have intervened on the first round if he had enough playing tricks for a sound overcall or enough points for some other course of action. With a limited hand he has to wait and see.

Sequence (e) A player who has already bid can reopen the bidding if the opponents have interfered and there has been no action from his partner. Thus:

West	North	East	South
1♠	2♣	NB	NB
?			

98

West can reopen now to prevent the bidding dying. If he makes a reopening double (always take-out in nature) in the example given above, he would be asking his partner to bid a red suit, or give delayed support for spades, or even to pass the double for penalties. We saw this useful device (the reopening double) in action on an earlier hand (p. 89).

The conclusion is that it's practically never worth letting the opponents play quietly in a fit at the two-level. If they have a fit, then you have a fit, and if they are stopping at the two level, you must have the strength to compete. If you compete, you may snatch the part-score yourself, or you may push the opponents to the three-level, which could be one too many. This competitive strategy has been developed at match point pairs play but it is good business too at rubber bridge or teams. However, be careful about the vulnerability, particularly at rubber and teams. Also at rubber bridge, make sure the opponents really have limited their hands and have not stopped bidding just because they have a part-score.

It is, of course, most important to ensure that the opponents *do* have a fit. Bidding such as 1♠ - 2♣, 2♠ - NB may be on misfitting hands, so you should not rush to intervene.

Here are a number of hands from competitions, which illustrate reopening bids in practice.

♠ 7 4 2	You are South, with both sides
♡ 9 4	vulnerable. Your partner, North,
♢ A 9 8 7 4 3	opens 1♣ and East intervenes with
♣ K 7	1♠. What do you bid?

In the absence of the overcall, you would have responded 1♢. However, you can't show the diamonds now because your partner might be forced to bid 3♣ if he had no fit for diamonds, and for all you know he may have a minimum opening bid. Nor can you respond 1NT as that would guarantee at least a partial stop in spades. So you are forced to pass.

So West passes and North doubles. East passes and it is up to you again. *Now* you can bid 2◇ in safety. Partner is likely to have reasonable support for any suit you bid.

The bidding:	*West*	*North*	*East*	*South*
		1♣	1♠	NB
	NB	Dbl	NB	2◇

The full deal:

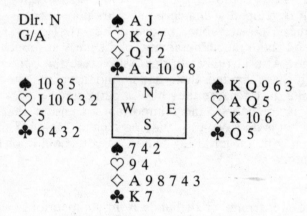

Dlr. N
G/A

North: ♠ A J ♡ K 8 7 ◇ Q J 2 ♣ A J 10 9 8

West: ♠ 10 8 5 ♡ J 10 6 3 2 ◇ 5 ♣ 6 4 3 2

East: ♠ K Q 9 6 3 ♡ A Q 5 ◇ K 10 6 ♣ Q 5

South: ♠ 7 4 2 ♡ 9 4 ◇ A 9 8 7 4 3 ♣ K 7

North-South have cruised to a very comfortable suit fit. They will go to 3◇ if their opponents persist with 2♠.

♠ Q 9 8 5
♡ A K 7
◇ A Q J 5 2
♣ 9

You are North, with neither side vulnerable. You deal and open 1◇. East over-calls with 2♣ and the next two players pass. What do you do now?

You would be happy if partner could be made to reveal some belated support for your suit, or to bid either hearts or spades, and the way to explore these exciting possibilities is by means of a reopening double. But what if partner's values are in the opponent's suit, clubs? That is even better. He will be able to pass your double, for penalties, and the result will be even more satisfying. In practice South bid 2♠, and that finished the auction.

The bidding:	West	North	East	South
		1◇	2♣	NB
	NB	Dbl	NB	2♠

The full deal:

Dlr. N
L/A

	♠ Q 9 8 5	
	♡ A K 7	
	◇ A Q J 5 2	
	♣ 9	

♠ 10 2		♠ A J 3
♡ J 6 5 4 3		♡ 9 2
◇ 7 4 3		◇ K 9 6
♣ Q 10 5		♣ A K J 6 2

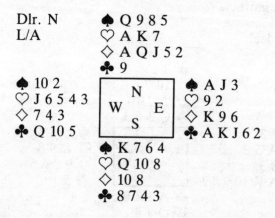

	♠ K 7 6 4	
	♡ Q 10 8	
	◇ 10 8	
	♣ 8 7 4 3	

Again, see how easy it is to find the right spot in this competitive auction. South held back because he didn't know where he was going, but North was able to make use of the flexible reopening double to find the spade fit. South is likely to have very little difficulty in the play.

♠ A K 10 5 You are South, dealer, with East-
♡ Q J 4   West vulnerable. You open 1♠,
◇ K Q 4 2 West over-calls with 2♣ and the next
♣ 4 2   two players pass. What do you bid
         now?

With fifteen high-card points and little defence to clubs,
you would like to compete further. It would be a mistake
to bid 2◇ because, by introducing a second suit, you
would be suggesting a hand with five spades and four
diamonds. As you have support for hearts and diamonds,
and would not object to playing in 2♠ if partner had
three, your best action, as on the previous two hands, is
to keep all options open with a double, and leave the
choice to partner.

The full deal:

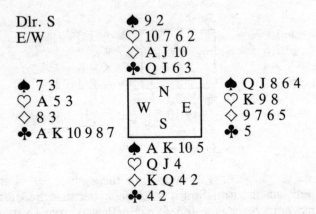

```
Dlr. S        ♠ 9 2
E/W           ♡ 10 7 6 2
              ◇ A J 10
              ♣ Q J 6 3
♠ 7 3                        ♠ Q J 8 6 4
♡ A 5 3       N              ♡ K 9 8
◇ 8 3      W     E           ◇ 9 7 6 5
♣ A K 10 9 8 7   S           ♣ 5
              ♠ A K 10 5
              ♡ Q J 4
              ◇ K Q 4 2
              ♣ 4 2
```

Partner has two choices now on his actual hand; he can
bid 2♡ or, alternatively, pass. If he bids 2♡ he can make
nine tricks, for a safe part-score. If he decides to pass 2♣
doubled he will convert South's reopening double into a
penalty double. With a good club holding, a dislike for
partner's spades and a safe spade lead, this may well be

the action he takes, particularly as the opponents are vulnerable. West is likely to lose two spade tricks, one heart, two diamonds and two clubs, so North-South will get an excellent result.

♠ A 4 3
♡ A K 9 4
♢ K Q J 10 3
♣ 4

You are North, dealer, with neither side vulnerable. You open 1♢, the next two players pass and West protects with a bid of 1NT. What do you bid now?

You have a good 17 high-card points and a strong suit but your partner has passed your opening bid and there is no hurry to get into the action again. If you defend you have an excellent lead against 1NT and, even if North makes a weakness conversion to 2 of a suit, your partner will know he should lead a diamond. Or partner may have long hearts or spades and a weak hand and be willing to show them over 1NT. For the moment just sit back and see what develops.

Now East retreats to 2♣ and the next two players pass, so the bidding has been:

West	North	East	South
	1♢	NB	NB
1NT	NB	2♣	NB
NB	?		

A contract of 2♣ is what you do *not* want to defend against and you can force partner to speak now by reopening the bidding with a take-out double. So you double 2♣ and your partner bids 2♠, which is where he plays the contract.

Dlr. N
L/A

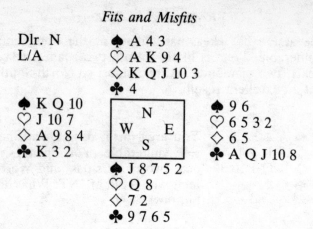

♠ A 4 3
♡ A K 9 4
◇ K Q J 10 3
♣ 4

♠ K Q 10
♡ J 10 7
◇ A 9 8 4
♣ K 3 2

♠ 9 6
♡ 6 5 3 2
◇ 6 5
♣ A Q J 10 8

♠ J 8 7 5 2
♡ Q 8
◇ 7 2
♣ 9 7 6 5

Against 2♠ by South, a trump lead is probably the best defence, as North-South have used a convention (the take-out double) to find their contract. However, South will be safe if he plays the contract with care.

♠ K 10 8 5 4
♡ J 4 2
◇ A
♣ 10 8 7 3

You are South, with East-West vulnerable. East opens 1♡. What do you bid?

You have a five-card spade suit but your hand lacks the four playing tricks needed for an immediate one-level overcall. Also there are some bad features, mainly the concentration of high cards in the short suits. You can't tell at this stage if the deal has misfitting features, for example, your partner may be short of spades and have long diamonds. Most significant of all, you don't know how strong the opponents are yet. Neither West nor East has limited his hand and you may be up against strong values. The final argument for not bidding now is that either West or North are likely to bid, so the auction will probably come back round to you again. You, therefore, pass and West responds 2♡, which is passed round to you. So the bidding has been:

West	North	East	South
		1♡	NB
2♡	NB	NB	?

Now the situation has changed completely. West has given a limited raise of his partner's suit and East has passed, so neither opponent can have great values, so your partner is marked with some strength. Also, when one side finds a suit fit, it increases the likelihood of a suit fit existing for the other side, which means that a reopening bid of 2♠ is now in order on the South hand.

The full deal:

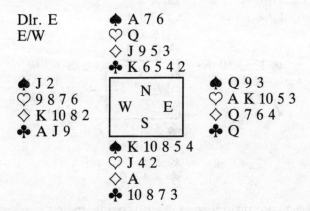

```
Dlr. E        ♠ A 7 6
E/W           ♡ Q
              ◇ J 9 5 3
              ♣ K 6 5 4 2

♠ J 2              N        ♠ Q 9 3
♡ 9 8 7 6     W         E   ♡ A K 10 5 3
◇ K 10 8 2         S        ◇ Q 7 6 4
♣ A J 9                     ♣ Q
              ♠ K 10 8 5 4
              ♡ J 4 2
              ◇ A
              ♣ 10 8 7 3
```

If East-West lead spades it will help South to play the suit, so he may make five spades and a trick in each of the other suits; if they don't lead spades, South will take two heart ruffs to make sure of his contract. If East-West continue to 3♡ they may go down, so North-South should resist the temptation to bid 3♠.

♠ K Q 10 9 8　You are West, with North-South
♡ K 9 3　　　vulnerable. You open 1♠, North
◇ 9 8　　　　over-calls with 2◇ and the next two
♣ A K 6　　　players pass. What do you bid?

Again, your hand is suitable for a reopening double, as
you would be happy to play clubs or hearts, if partner
holds one or both of these suits. In practice, your partner
puts you back to spades. So the bidding has been:

West	North	East	South
1♠	2◇	NB	NB
Dbl	NB	2♠	

The full deal:

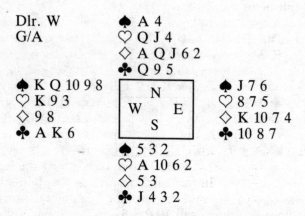

```
Dlr. W          ♠ A 4
G/A             ♡ Q J 4
                ◇ A Q J 6 2
                ♣ Q 9 5
♠ K Q 10 9 8   ┌─────────┐   ♠ J 7 6
♡ K 9 3        │    N    │   ♡ 8 7 5
◇ 9 8          │ W     E │   ◇ K 10 7 4
♣ A K 6        │    S    │   ♣ 10 8 7
                └─────────┘
                ♠ 5 3 2
                ♡ A 10 6 2
                ◇ 5 3
                ♣ J 4 3 2
```

The hand produced a useful swing in a teams-of-four
match. In one room the bidding was as shown above, and
East-West made eight tricks. In the other room, North
made the better choice of a double of 1♠, and South bid
and managed to make 2♡.

Are East-West always booked for a bad result if North
makes the right choice of a double of 1♠? No, they
should not be. If the bidding goes:

West	North	East	South
1♠	Dbl	NB	2♡
?			

West should not go on (he has bid his hand, and North is still unlimited) but when North passes, *East* can bid 2♠, as the opponents have found a fit and have stopped at the 2-level.

♠ J 3
♡ K Q 10 9 8
♢ 9 6 4 2
♣ Q 10

You are South, with North-South vulnerable. Your left hand opponent, West, opens 1♢ and the next two players pass. Do you protect?

With such a good suit and eight points you are certainly strong enough to make a protective bid of 1♡, but the question is, should you do so on this particular hand? There is one unsatisfactory feature about the hand, and that is the presence of four diamonds, the suit your opponent has bid. Ask yourself the questions, 'What will happen if I pass, and what will happen if I bid?' If you pass, the play of 1♢ may be made slightly awkward for declarer by the presence of your four trumps; even if made, it will not score much for East-West. If you bid 1♡ and play there, you may be in difficulty if the hearts are misfitting too. In fact you are probably only likely to play in 1♡ if this contract suits the opponents, and you are vulnerable so it will be costly to go down. Finally, your intervention gives the opponents the chance to bid again and they may improve their contract. For instance, if East has five or six spades and a weak hand, he could bid 1♠ when it comes round to him, in perfect safety, because his hand is limited by his original failure to respond. It is clear, therefore, that there is much more to be lost than gained and you should stay out of the action.

The full deal:

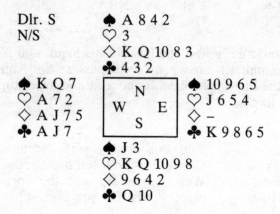

Dlr. S
N/S

♠ A 8 4 2
♡ 3
◇ K Q 10 8 3
♣ 4 3 2

♠ K Q 7
♡ A 7 2
◇ A J 7 5
♣ A J 7

♠ 10 9 6 5
♡ J 6 5 4
◇ —
♣ K 9 8 6 5

♠ J 3
♡ K Q 10 9 8
◇ 9 6 4 2
♣ Q 10

When the hand occurred at a recent congress, there was a wide variety of results. Some Easts dragged up a response and West jumped to 3NT, not an easy contract. West players who were left to play in 1◇ also had a miserable time. A few Souths played in 1♡ but, because of the lack of entries to the South hand, the contract proved too difficult. Some of the best scores for East-West occurred when South *did* intervene with a protective 1♡; this gave West the chance to bid 1NT (or to double 1♡) and allowed East to take out into 2♣ for a safe part-score.

♠ J 8 3
♡ 10 6
◇ A 9 6 5
♣ K 7 5 4

You are South, with neither side vulnerable. Your partner, North, opens 1♡. What do you respond?

Your hand is suitable for a response of 1NT, being balanced, lacking support for partner's suit and in the 6-9 high-card point range. You bid 1NT, West passes, your partner passes and East comes in with 2♣. You pass,

West passes, your partner doubles and East passes. So the bidding has been:

North	East	South	West
1♡	NB	1NT	NB
NB	2♠	NB	NB
Dbl	NB	?	

What do you bid now? Does partner want to punish 2♠ or is he trying to get you to bid a suit (you have not shown either of your minors) by employing a double that is take-out in principle? Let's look at the full deal:

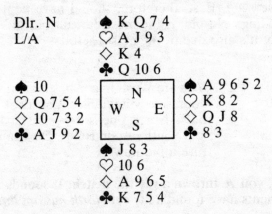

```
Dlr. N          ♠ K Q 7 4
L/A             ♡ A J 9 3
                ◇ K 4
                ♣ Q 10 6

♠ 10                        ♠ A 9 6 5 2
♡ Q 7 5 4          N        ♡ K 8 2
◇ 10 7 3 2      W     E      ◇ Q J 8
♣ A J 9 2          S        ♣ 8 3

                ♠ J 8 3
                ♡ 10 6
                ◇ A 9 6 5
                ♣ K 7 5 4
```

The answer becomes clear when you see all the hands. Partner is doubling for penalties. East may well lose three spade tricks, two hearts, two diamonds and a club. North has handled the auction correctly, opening 1♡ with 4-4 in the majors and too many points to open 1NT, passing your response of 1NT because there is little chance of game and seizing the chance of a good score by doubling 2♠.

So how should South *know* that North's is a penalty double? Well, he has to remember that East has merely reopened the bidding; he did not bid first time round, he is not strong and he is merely competing for the part score. Also, South *has* shown his suit. His 'suit' is no-trumps. Partner knows that, so the double is for business. It is rather like the situation where a player has opened 1NT, showing a balanced hand and a defined points range, and can then leave further decisions to his partner.

What did East do wrong? He should have appreciated that, although North-South have stopped bidding, North could pass on up to 15 points in this sequence and that South could have as many as nine. More important still, his opponents had *not* announced a fit; the no-trump response to one of a suit can include some grisly misfits, as we have seen. East, therefore, should have kept out of the bidding. 'No bid' is the most difficult bid to learn to use, but it's also one of the most useful!

♠ K 10 8 4 2   You are West, in a teams match, with
♡ K 10 7   your side vulnerable. You deal and
◇ J 9   pass. North opens 1♣, East passes
♣ K 9 3   and South responds 2♣. Do you ven-
                ture a bid now?

If you do, you've thrown away the match. It sounds as if the opponents have found a fit, but *North has not limited his hand*.

The full deal:

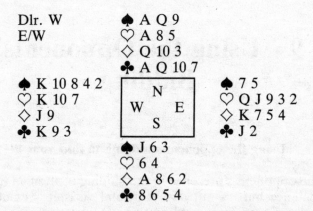

Dlr. W ♠ A Q 9
E/W ♡ A 8 5
◇ Q 10 3
♣ A Q 10 7

♠ K 10 8 4 2   ♠ 7 5
♡ K 10 7   ♡ Q J 9 3 2
◇ J 9   ◇ K 7 5 4
♣ K 9 3   ♣ J 2

♠ J 6 3
♡ 6 4
◇ A 8 6 2
♣ 8 6 5 4

North opened 1♣, intending to rebid 2NT. East passed and South got in the way with 2♣, a rather pre-emptive effort. In practice, West foolishly bid 2♠ even though North was unlimited, and North fell upon the contract with a penalty double.

In the play, West made only five tricks, so he was three down, doubled and vulnerable. And he was lucky . . . the spades broke 3 - 3.

9 Using the Opponents' Bidding

Using the opponent's bidding to find your fit

The opponent's presence in the bidding is often an inconvenience but it's not always a total disaster. Sometimes one can turn their bidding to your own advantage. For example, you will not be displeased, on the three hands below, if, before you have the chance to speak, your opponent opens 1♢ in front of you.

(a) ♠ K Q J 10 3	(b) ♠ A 4	(c) ♠ A J 8 3
♡ K 4	♡ K Q 7 3	♡ Q J 9 4
♢ 5 4 2	♢ K 10 8 3	♢ 5
♣ 10 7 5	♣ K J 8	♣ A J 6 3
Bid 1♠	Bid 1NT	Double

In each case the 1♢ opening has simplified your task. In fact, hands (a) and (c) would be difficult to describe without it.

In an uncontested auction there are many situations where you *have* to keep the bidding open. For example, when you open with a suit, you promise a rebid. But when the opponents interfere you may have the chance to pass on a limited hand when you don't know where you are going, or where you suspect a misfit, knowing that the bidding will get back round to partner. This type of opportunity to hang back is often missed by unthinking bidders, so some examples are given later in the chapter.

Making the most of opponents' misfits

We have already seen how one can double opponent's artificial bid to show a suit of your own (p. 50). But what if their artificial bid shows *two* suits, such as the unusual no-trump bid? A simple but effective method is to use a double in this situation to show the ability to double *one* of their suits. Your partner should be able to work out which one. Now, if the hands are fitting badly, you should be able to extract a good penalty from opponents instead of blundering about. For example:

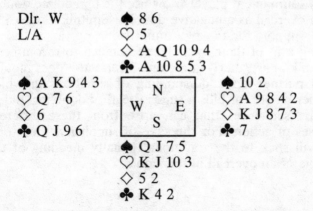

Dlr. W
L/A

♠ 8 6
♡ 5
♢ A Q 10 9 4
♣ A 10 8 5 3

♠ A K 9 4 3
♡ Q 7 6
♢ 6
♣ Q J 9 6

♠ 10 2
♡ A 9 8 4 2
♢ K J 8 7 3
♣ 7

♠ Q J 7 5
♡ K J 10 3
♢ 5 2
♣ K 4 2

West opens 1♠ and North bids 2NT (unusual, both minors). East now doubles to show the ability to double one of their suits, so when South bids 3♣, West can double, and there is no escape for North-South.

There are also some punishing sequences that can arise after an opponent has made a take-out double, if the hands turn out to be misfitting after all. We said on p. 47 that a redouble by opener's partner showed good values (at least 9 points) without primary support for partner's suit. In the example given, your partner opened 1♠, the next player doubled and you redoubled on ♠K 9 6, ♡K 9 6, ◇K 9 6 4, ♣Q 10 3. Your side has the balance of points and you are ready to double the opponents if they get too high.

Remember, the opener must co-operate with his partner (the redoubler) if the partnership is to get the best out of these sequences. Thus he would bid on with a weak, shapely hand, pass a bid from the doubler's partner on an average hand, and double such a bid with good defence and 3 or more trumps (see p. 47).

Traditionally, the immediate double of an overcall is for penalties showing dislike of partner's suit, liking for opponent's suit and general defensive strength. However, many tournament players now use the immediate double of an overcall as a negative double ('Sputnik' double) to show support for the two unbid suits, i.e. as an aid to finding a fit of their own. There is much to recommend 'Sputnik', particularly at the one-level, but it does require good partnership understanding of situations in which partner passes, or bids a suit, instead of doubling and of all the sequences that can arise from these different courses of action. For the sake of simplicity, therefore, we will stick to the traditional penalty meaning of the double of an overcall in this book.

The following hands from competitions are all concerned with using the opponents' bidding, and making the most of their misfits.

♠ 10
♡ Q 9 7 5
◇ A Q 9
♣ K 10 7 5 2

You are East, with North-South vulnerable. Your partner, West, deals and opens 1♠. North overcalls with 2◇. What do you bid?

114

Using the Opponents' Bidding·

You have the three requirements for the penalty double of an overcall, namely dislike of partner's suit, liking for opponent's suit (your diamond honours are well placed) and general defensive strength. If your double is passed out you will have no problem with the opening lead, as you will lead the singleton of your partner's suit.

The full deal:

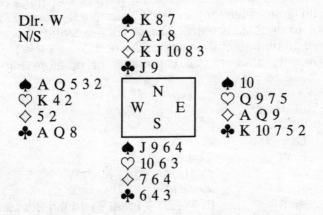

Dlr. W
N/S

♠ K 8 7
♡ A J 8
◇ K J 10 8 3
♣ J 9

♠ A Q 5 3 2
♡ K 4 2
◇ 5 2
♣ A Q 8

♠ 10
♡ Q 9 7 5
◇ A Q 9
♣ K 10 7 5 2

♠ J 9 6 4
♡ 10 6 3
◇ 7 6 4
♣ 6 4 3

The defence should have no trouble in taking a spade trick, a spade ruff, two clubs, two trump tricks and a heart, to put declarer at least two down.

Postscript: North's overcall is unsound, particularly when vulnerable. Although East-West can make a game, East could not be sure of that, and so he preferred to double and 'take the money'.

♠ 2
♡ A 10 6
◇ K 9 7 6
♣ K J 8 5 3

You are West with East-West vulnerable. Your partner opens 1♠ and South overcalls with 2♡. What do you bid?

Again, you have the three requirements for the penalty double of an overcall, i.e. dislike of partner's suit, liking for the opponent's suit and general defensive values. True, your liking for the opponent's suit is not as great as on the last hand but your dislike for partner's suit is very pronounced. It is a pity that it's your side that is vulnerable, not theirs, and it's just possible that you may miss a vulnerable game. However, the chance of this happening is much reduced when partner's opening bid has hit your singleton, so from your point of view it's better to double. If partner has a very exceptional hand he can go on bidding. Your penalty double of a low level contract is, after all, an expression of opinion, not a command to pass.

The full deal:

```
Dlr. N          ♠ A 8 5
E/W             ♡ 4 3
                ◇ 10 8 4 3 2
                ♣ Q 10 9

♠ 2                          ♠ Q 10 9 7 4 3
♡ A 10 6          N          ♡ 7 2
◇ K 9 7 6     W     E        ◇ A J
♣ K J 8 5 3       S          ♣ A 6 4

                ♠ K J 6
                ♡ K Q J 9 8 5
                ◇ Q 5
                ♣ 7 2
```

As explained on p. 49, partner will judge whether or not to remove the double by looking at the number of trumps that he holds. With two or more trumps he will almost always leave the double in, so he will pass on this hand. If he had a void in hearts he would usually take the double out as he would judge that it is declarer, rather than West, who has great length in the suit. With a singleton trump he will leave the double in if his hand is suitable for defence, i.e. if a considerable part of his strength is in the side suits and particularly if he has tricks that will develop quickly, that is, aces and kings, rather than queens and jacks. On the hand shown on p. 116, although he has only eleven high-card points, he is almost perfect for defence, having two hearts, two outside aces and few points wasted in the spade suit. After the bidding 1♠-2♡-Dbl-All pass, the defence is fairly easy. West leads his singleton spade to the ♣5, ♠7 and ♣J. South leads a trump, West goes up with the ace and gets two spade ruffs by putting his partner on lead twice in the minor suits. The two minor suit kings then ensure that the contract goes two down.

♠ 9 2
♡ K J 6 3
♢ J 10 9 5 2
♣ A 10

You are South, with neither side vulnerable. Your partner, North, opens 1NT (12-14 points) and East overcalls with 2♡. What do you bid?

Even if partner has only 12 points, your side is stronger than the opponents and you can see that the hearts lie badly for East, so 2♡ is unlikely to make. Of course, it will make *sometimes* so you may not wish to risk doubling the opponents into game at rubber bridge or teams. At duplicate pairs, however, the probability that the contract will go down makes the penalty double an irresistible proposition. What is more you have a good lead, the top-of-sequence ♢J. When you have a sound trump holding such as K-J-x-x, you should lead your long suit, to force declarer to ruff, and so shorten his trumps, until he has less trumps than you.

117

Fits and Misfits

The full deal:

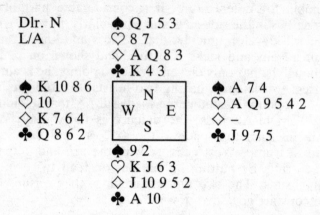

Dlr. N
L/A

♠ Q J 5 3
♡ 8 7
♢ A Q 8 3
♣ K 4 3

♠ K 10 8 6
♡ 10
♢ K 7 6 4
♣ Q 8 6 2

♠ A 7 4
♡ A Q 9 5 4 2
♢ –
♣ J 9 7 5

♠ 9 2
♡ K J 6 3
♢ J 10 9 5 2
♣ A 10

East will probably trump the diamond lead. He may enter
dummy with the ♠K and finesse the ♡Q. South will win
and lead another diamond. If East trumps again the hand
will become very dangerous for him, as his trumps will
now be reduced to the same number as South's. It only
requires the defence to lead one more diamond and they
are likely to take trump control, and still have diamonds
to cash. East will probably make only three diamond
ruffs, the ♡A and two top spades, to be two down.

♠ 8
♡ 7 5
♢ 9 7 6 5
♣ K J 9 8 6 5

You are North, with neither side
vulnerable. Your partner, South,
opens 1♡ and West overcalls with
2♣. What do you do now?

You would dearly love to double 2♣ for penalties but
you must not fall into the trap of doing so. There are
three requirements for a penalty double in this situation,
namely dislike of partner's suit, liking for the opponent's
suit and general defensive strength. You have the first

two requirements but not the last, so you must pass and hope East passes too. You have no problem with the opening lead, your partner's suit, the ♡7.

The full deal:

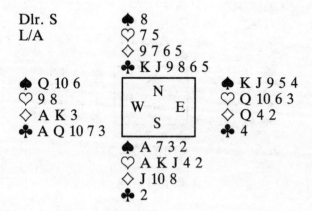

Dlr. S
L/A

North:
♠ 8
♡ 7 5
♢ 9 7 6 5
♣ K J 9 8 6 5

West:
♠ Q 10 6
♡ 9 8
♢ A K 3
♣ A Q 10 7 3

East:
♠ K J 9 5 4
♡ Q 10 6 3
♢ Q 4 2
♣ 4

South:
♠ A 7 3 2
♡ A K J 4 2
♢ J 10 8
♣ 2

2♣ was decimated, of course, on the marked heart lead. South won with the ♡J, played ♡K and another, for North to ruff. Then a spade to the ♠A and ♡A left West with nothing worth discarding and a fistful of clubs to lose. Although it might be thought that 2♣ *doubled* would be even more satisfactory for North-South, it's a mistake to double on the North hand. Your double will induce East to rescue into 2♠ and South will double, thinking you have general defensive values. You can see that the contract of 2♠ doubled makes with the greatest of ease, and you will have turned a potential triumph into a certain disaster. Another possibility is that, after 1♡-2♣-NB-NB, South may reopen with a take-out double, but if East escapes to 2♠, it will not be doubled.

Postscript: Many Wests would have preferred to double rather than bid 2♣, even though the double of 1♡ more usually shows four spades. East could hardly be blamed for not rescuing West from 2♣ into 2♠; he was entitled to expect a more robust club suit from his partner.

Here is a hand which decided a close teams-of-4 match.

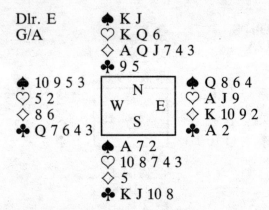

Dlr. E
G/A

♠ K J
♡ K Q 6
♢ A Q J 7 4 3
♣ 9 5

♠ 10 9 5 3
♡ 5 2
♢ 8 6
♣ Q 7 6 4 3

♠ Q 8 6 4
♡ A J 9
♢ K 10 9 2
♣ A 2

♠ A 7 2
♡ 10 8 7 4 3
♢ 5
♣ K J 10 8

With both sides vulnerable, East dealt and opened 1NT (12-14 points). In one room this was passed round to North, who doubled for penalties (North needs to be full value for his double in this position as West may have passed with up to ten points). The next two players passed and West ran to 2♣. North now bid 2♢, to show his suit, and South, with the clubs well stopped and facing strong bidding from his partner, tried 3NT. A spade was led and, with the major suit high cards sitting badly and the diamonds not breaking, North-South were forced to concede 200 points. They were not too pleased to learn that their team mates had also lost 200, on the East-West cards.

In the other room the bidding started exactly the same with 1NT by East-NB-NB-Dbl by North. East and South again passed and West ran to 2♣ as before. The difference came now. North in the other room took the view that he had already shown his hand with his double of

1NT and was content for his partner to take any further decisions. So he passed, East passed and South fell upon 2♣ with a penalty double. Although the defence was not perfect, this still went one off.

Postscript: Having shown his values on the first round of bidding, North's reticence on the second round enabled his side to take full advantage of the misfit. Many tournament players have the agreement that if the opponents run from 1NT doubled, then any pass by the doubling side is forcing on partner to take some action. Such a forcing pass would have to be alerted, of course. The subject is well covered in Eric Crowhurst's *Acol in Competition*.

♠ 6 2	You are South, dealer, with both
♡ A Q 10 7 5	sides vulnerable. What is your open-
◇ K Q J	ing bid?
♣ 9 6 4	

With 12 high-card points and a good five-card suit you should open the bidding. Although, in theory, you could open 1NT with this shape, the concentration of points into two suits make it more suitable for a bid of 1♡. West now passes, your partner responds 1♠ and East overcalls with 2♣. What do you bid now?

If East had not intervened you would have been prepared to rebid 2♡, for when you open with a suit call, you promise a rebid. Now that East has intervened, however, the bidding will get back round to partner and so you no longer have this obligation. If you could have supported spades for example, or if your hearts were longer or if you could have offered partner a biddable second suit, you would have been pleased to bid on, but on this very ordinary hand you can afford to sit back and wait. You need not worry that you have not shown five hearts. If partner has as many as three hearts he can put you back to hearts now, and if he is short of hearts you will be glad that you didn't bid blindly on.

The full deal:

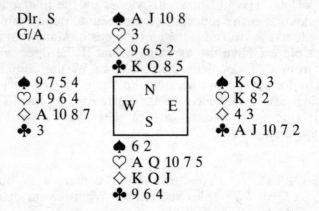

Dlr. S
G/A

North:
♠ A J 10 8
♡ 3
◇ 9 6 5 2
♣ K Q 8 5

West:
♠ 9 7 5 4
♡ J 9 6 4
◇ A 10 8 7
♣ 3

East:
♠ K Q 3
♡ K 8 2
◇ 4 3
♣ A J 10 7 2

South:
♠ 6 2
♡ A Q 10 7 5
◇ K Q J
♣ 9 6 4

You pass 2♣, West also passes and North, with eleven points and a complete misfit for your suit pounces on the 2♣ bid with a double. As there is no suit East-West can escape to, 2♣ doubled becomes the final contract. Declarer will be lucky to make more than six tricks, resulting in a substantial penalty.

Postscript: A wooden 2♡ rebid from South would have deprived his side of the opportunity of a good plus score and pitched North-South into trouble instead.

♠ 6 5 2
♡ K Q 8 7 2
◇ K J
♣ A Q 4

You are West, with neither side vulnerable. You open 1♡, North doubles and East redoubles. South now bids 2♣. What do you do now?

Your partner's redouble shows 9+ points, no more than three hearts and an interest in doubling the opponents. However, as explained on p. 00, these redoubling sequences can often go wrong if the opener doesn't help his partner. With sound opening values and with A-Q-4 of trumps you must double to show that your hand is suitable for defence.

The full deal:

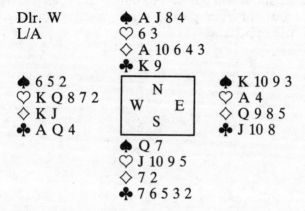

```
Dlr. W          ♠ A J 8 4
L/A             ♡ 6 3
                ◇ A 10 6 4 3
                ♣ K 9
  ♠ 6 5 2              ♠ K 10 9 3
  ♡ K Q 8 7 2          ♡ A 4
  ◇ K J               ◇ Q 9 8 5
  ♣ A Q 4              ♣ J 10 8
                ♠ Q 7
                ♡ J 10 9 5
                ◇ 7 2
                ♣ 7 6 5 3 2
```

If North rescues into diamonds or spades, East will be able to double and East-West should collect a healthy penalty bonus.

We should not like you to think that we approve of the take-out double on the North hand. Even so, it is easy for East-West to go wrong. If West fails to co-operate with his partner by doubling 2♣, and passes instead, East will not know what to do when 2♣ comes round to him.

In the lower echelons of bridge hardly anyone dares to double a contract lower than a game or slam, but in the previous pages we have seen plenty of profitable doubles of low level contracts, one of the signs that your bridge is progressing from learner to player level.

The key feature of hands where a low level penalty double works is that they are all *misfits* and the defending side has at least its fair share of points. If, in contrast, you have a *fit* with your partner, then the low level penalty double will not work. As pointed out on p. 48 the more cards you have in your partner's suit, the less will the opponents have, so they will have less losers when they play the contract. In short, if you have a fit, then they have a fit, and it will pay you to bid on as far as you dare in your own or your partner's suit before stopping to double the opponents.

10 Defence Against Fits

In this chapter we shall assume that the opponents have won the contract and that we, as defenders, have to defeat them if we can. Some of the defensive weapons that will help us are mentioned briefly below, with examples of these methods in action, later in the chapter.

Signals and discards

It is impossible to defend effectively without the use of some standard defensive signals. The three that are listed below should be familiar to most players.

1 *The attitude signal.*

The most important signal of all, when *partner leads* a suit, is to tell him whether you like it or not, by playing *high to encourage*, or *low to discourage*.

2 *The length signal.*

When *declarer leads* a suit (from his own hand or dummy), a defender may play *high-low* to show an *even* number of cards in that suit, but play his cards upwards (*low first*) to show an *odd* number of cards.

3 *The discard signal.*

When *discarding*, different players have different methods. The traditional method is to discard a high card from a suit to show an interest, and a low card to show no interest, in that suit.

And now for some others that may not be so familiar:

4 *The suit preference signal (SPS)*

In addition to the standard signals given above are the

more specialised *suit preference signals* (Lavinthal or McKenney suit preference signals) in which the play of a card of one suit gives information about another suit. These signals come into their own when a defender knows that his partner is going to switch suits anyway, and can indicate what he would like him to switch to.

For example, against a trump contract, if a defender leads the ace of a side suit and there is a singleton of that suit in dummy, it is obvious that the defender will switch to another suit. His partner can help him to make the right choice by playing a high card to indicate an interest in a high-ranking suit or a low card to indicate an interest in a low-ranking suit. The trump suit is always excluded from the choice, so there can be no ambiguity.

Similarly, if a defender is leading a suit that he knows his partner can trump, he can couple it with a suit preference signal by playing a higher than necessary card of the suit to indicate that he would like his partner to return the higher ranking of the remaining suits. Thus if South were declarer in a spade contract and if, at some stage, West led a higher than necessary heart for East to trump, he would be indicating that his partner should return a diamond, not a club.

Many players extend the principle of Lavinthal or McKenney suit preference signals to their *discards* also, and there is much to be said for this, but in this book we shall stick to standard methods for the discard signals described above and restrict suit preference signals to the two types of situation just mentioned.

5 *The trump 'peter'*

The trump 'peter', i.e. the play of a high card followed by a low card in the trump suit, has a special meaning. It shows precisely three trumps and a shortage in a side suit, that is, a desire to ruff.

Other defensive information

Every time you lead a suit, you give some information about your holding in it, because there is a convention attaching to all leads, (e.g. top of a sequence, top of a doubleton, low from an honour, middle-up-down from three small, etc.).

Sometimes the declarer will attempt to scramble your signals by making an unusual play (a 'false' card) in the suit your side has led. In cases where there appears to be a conflict between the information coming from partner and from declarer, it will pay you to trust your partner. Even if occasionally he turns out to be wrong, it will be better to accept the occasional mishap, rather than to erode partnership confidence by showing that you don't trust him.

Trump promotion

At times the defenders, each with a rather flimsy trump holding, can gang up on declarer in the trump suit, and squeeze an extra defensive trick by a 'trump promotion'. The classic case is where the trumps are distributed thus:

```
            x x x
          ┌───────┐
          │   N   │
  Q x     │ W   E │     J x
          │   S   │
          └───────┘
          A K x x x x
```

South is declarer, and can normally drop the defender's trumps with the ace and king. However, if before he can do so, West leads a suit that both East and South can trump, then East's jack will force out a high card from South, and West's queen will be promoted. Similarly:

```
            A K x x x x
          ┌───────┐
          │   N   │
  10 9 8  │ W   E │     J
          │   S   │
          └───────┘
             Q x x
```

If West can lead a suit that both North and East can trump, North will have to trump high and West's 10 will be promoted.

Now for some examples from play:

♠ A K J 8 5 4 3 You are West, with neither side
♥ 9 6   vulnerable. What is your opening
♦ 8 6   bid?
♣ 9 5

You should make six or seven tricks so a pre-emptive 3♠ is in order. North bids 3NT for take-out, your partner passes and South bids 5♣.

The bidding:	*West*	*North*	*East*	*South*
	3♠	3NT	NB	5♣

You lead the ♠A and dummy goes down:

Dlr. W   ♠ 10 7
L/A   ♥ K 10 7 5 3
              ♦ A K J 7
              ♣ A J

♠ A K J 8 5 4 3
♥ 9 6
♦ 8 6
♣ 9 5

On your ♠A dummy plays ♠7, East plays ♠2 and South plays ♠Q. What do you do now?

It is unlikely that partner has a doubleton spade, or he would have started a 'peter' (high-low); either partner has ♠ 9-6-2 and declarer has the singleton ♠Q (quite likely), or else partner has the singleton ♠2 and declarer has false-carded from ♠ Q-9-6 (unlikely, unless South

128

is particularly devious). East has discouraged spades by playing his cards upwards. He has not given a suit preference signal; the encouraging/discouraging signal on partner's lead takes preference over all other signals. You must switch, but you will have to guess which suit to switch to. Declarer may be able to take discards on dummy's diamonds so you must try to take your defensive tricks quickly. A heart is the only hope, and you should lead ♡9, the top of your doubleton.

The full deal:

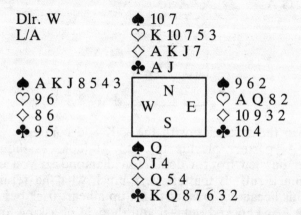

```
Dlr. W            ♠ 10 7
L/A               ♡ K 10 7 5 3
                  ◇ A K J 7
                  ♣ A J
♠ A K J 8 5 4 3        N         ♠ 9 6 2
♡ 9 6          W            E    ♡ A Q 8 2
◇ 8 6                 S          ◇ 10 9 3 2
♣ 9 5                           ♣ 10 4
                  ♠ Q
                  ♡ J 4
                  ◇ Q 5 4
                  ♣ K Q 8 7 6 3 2
```

On this simple defence East-West take the first three tricks. If West can't trust his partner's signals, however, he may try to cash a second spade; declarer will ruff, draw trumps and throw a heart loser on the fourth diamond.

```
♠ A 9 7           You are East, dealer, with both sides
♡ K Q             vulnerable. You open 1◇ and South
◇ A K 10 3        overcalls 2♣. The next two hands
♣ 10 8 4 3        pass. What do you bid now?
```

Although you have 16 high-card points, your hand has

several bad features. You have too much strength concentrated in the short suits and you have four cards in the suit that your opponent has bid. Partner is weak and, as you are vulnerable, it is best to go quietly and pass – another example of not bidding just because you've got points.

West leads the ◇6 against South's contract of 2♣ and dummy goes down:

Dlr. E ♠ K J 10 6
G/A   ♡ A 10 3
    ◇ J 5 2
    ♣ 7 6 2

        ♠ A 9 7
        ♡ K Q
        ◇ A K 10 3
        ♣ 10 8 4 3

You win the first trick with the ◇K and continue with the ◇A, partner playing the ◇4. It looks as though partner has led from a doubleton diamond so you can give him a ruff. It matters very much what he returns after this because you want to set up a heart trick before your ♠A is knocked out – if you thought of asking for a spade, think again. You can't give West a second ruff if he *does* put you in with the ♠A because he can't have started with more than a singleton trump. Why? South overcalled your one diamond with two clubs, marking him with a five-card club suit, which leaves only a singleton for West. There's a lot more to think of when you embark on a hand of bridge than you may have realised! So you must lead the ◇3, this low card being a suit preference signal, indicating that you want him to return the lower ranking of the two remaining suits (excluding trumps).

The full deal:

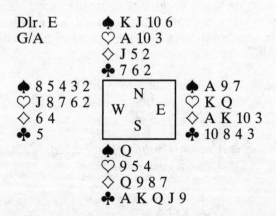

Dlr. E ♠ K J 10 6
G/A ♡ A 10 3
◇ J 5 2
♣ 7 6 2

♠ 8 5 4 3 2 ♠ A 9 7
♡ J 8 7 6 2 ♡ K Q
◇ 6 4 ◇ A K 10 3
♣ 5 ♣ 10 8 4 3

♠ Q
♡ 9 5 4
◇ Q 9 8 7
♣ A K Q J 9

So the defence makes two diamonds and a diamond ruff, and the switch to a heart ensures a heart trick in addition to the ♠A. Although 2♣ was just made, this result was worth only 4 out of 20 match points for North-South when it was played in a duplicate event. Some Easts, having failed to count the club suit, had thoughtlessly asked for a spade return by playing the ◇10 for West to ruff. Other East-West pairs had continued bidding but failed to make their contracts, East's fault, because his hand really did not merit pressing on. Yet others had pushed their opponents into no-trumps when they should have kept quiet instead of giving North-South the chance of a better score.

♠ K 10 9 8 6 2   You are East with neither side
♡ 6   vulnerable. Your right-hand op-
◇ K 10 2   ponent, (North) opens 1♣. What do
♣ A 8 6   you bid?

You are likely to make four spade tricks and a trick and a half in the minor suits so you can certainly overcall with

131

1♠. This is the time to come into the bidding; you have
a six-card suit so you should not come to much harm,
and your intervention deprives the opposition of bidding
space. However, South bids 2♡, your partner passes and
North bids 4♡.

The bidding:

	West	North	East	South
		1♣	1♠	2♡
	NB	4♡		

*West leads the ♠A against South's contract of 4♡ and
dummy goes down:*

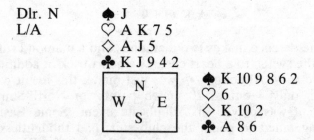

Dlr. N
L/A

♠ J
♡ A K 7 5
♢ A J 5
♣ K J 9 4 2

♠ K 10 9 8 6 2
♡ 6
♢ K 10 2
♣ A 8 6

Which card do you play to the first trick?

With a singleton spade in dummy, there is no point in
partner continuing with this suit, so you know that he
will switch. You can make a suit preference signal to
show him which suit you would like him to switch to. The
♣A will probably make a trick anyway, so you don't
want a club, you want a diamond, to set up some winners
whilst you still have the ♣A as an entry. You must play
a high spade, as a suit preference signal for the higher
ranking of the remaining suits (excluding the trump suit).
You can't afford to play the ♠K under your partner's
ace, as declarer may have the ♠Q, so the ♠10 will have
to do.

The full deal:

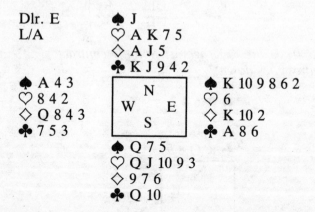

Dlr. E
L/A

♠ J
♡ A K 7 5
◇ A J 5
♣ K J 9 4 2

♠ A 4 3
♡ 8 4 2
◇ Q 8 4 3
♣ 7 5 3

N
W   E
S

♠ K 10 9 8 6 2
♡ 6
◇ K 10 2
♣ A 8 6

♠ Q 7 5
♡ Q J 10 9 3
◇ 9 7 6
♣ Q 10

When he sees your ♠10 partner will switch to the ◇3.
If dummy's ◇5 is played, the ◇10 will hold the trick and
a diamond can be returned to force out dummy's ace,
which will ensure a total of four tricks for the defence.

♠ 8 3
♡ 9 7 3
◇ J 8 5 4 3
♣ J 8 5

You are East, with North-South
vulnerable. Your left hand opponent
(South) opens 1♡, your partner
doubles for take-out and North
redoubles. What do you bid?

Some players believe that, in this situation, you should
pass and leave the decision to partner. However, partner
has asked for your suit, so you may as well help him out.
After 1♡-double-redouble *any* bid you make is weak so
there should be no harm in expressing a clear opinion.
You, therefore, bid 2◇, the suit you much prefer. Now
South bids 2♡, showing a long heart suit in a weak
opening hand (see p. 47), your partner passes and North
tries 3♡ (a rather undisciplined bid), which is passed out.

The bidding:

South	West	North	East
1♡	Dbl	Redbl	2◇
2♡	NB	3♡	All pass

West leads the ♠K *against South's contract of 3♡ and dummy goes down:*

♠ A 6 4 2
♡ J 6
◇ Q 9 2
♣ K Q 8 7

♠ 8 3
♡ 9 7 3
◇ J 8 5 4 3
♣ J 6 5

Declarer puts up dummy's ♠A and leads ♡J to your partner's ♡A. On the first trick you must play the ♠8 to indicate that you want the suit to be continued. On the ♡J you must play the ♡9, petering to show three trumps and a desire to ruff. Partner will now continue with the ♠Q and the ♠9 (a McKenney suit preference signal) so that, when you ruff, you will return a diamond instead of a club.

The full deal:

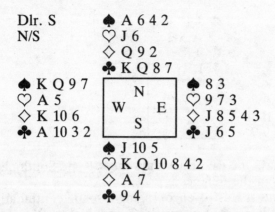

Dlr. S   ♠ A 6 4 2
N/S   ♡ J 6
         ◇ Q 9 2
         ♣ K Q 8 7

♠ K Q 9 7   ♠ 8 3
♡ A 5   ♡ 9 7 3
◇ K 10 6   ◇ J 8 5 4 3
♣ A 10 3 2   ♣ J 6 5

         ♠ J 10 5
         ♡ K Q 10 8 4 2
         ◇ A 7
         ♣ 9 4

You return the ◇4 (fourth highest), the fourth defensive signal on this hand, to establish the ◇K for partner and ensure that the contract goes one down.

♠ A K 7 2   You are West, with neither side
♡ 10 9 7   vulnerable. South, the dealer, opens
◇ A 10 4   1♡, and over his partner's response
♣ 10 9 7   of 2♣, rebids 2♡. North now jumps
              to 4♡.

So the bidding has gone:

North	South
	1♡
2♣	2♡
4♡	

What do you lead?

    As there is the risk of discards on dummy's clubs, you must try to take your winners in the side suits quickly, so you lead the ♠A.

Dummy goes down:

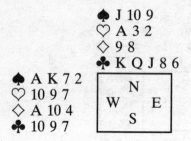

♠ J 10 9
♡ A 3 2
◇ 9 8
♣ K Q J 8 6

♠ A K 7 2
♡ 10 9 7
◇ A 10 4
♣ 10 9 7

Dummy plays the ♣9, East plays the ♣8 and South plays the ♣3. Plan the defence.

It looks as if East is encouraging a spade continuation so he must have ♠Q or possibly a doubleton. You continue with the ♠K and then the ♠7, your highest remaining spade, a suit preference signal to indicate that you want partner to return the higher ranking suit (excluding trumps), i.e. a diamond rather than a club.

The full deal:

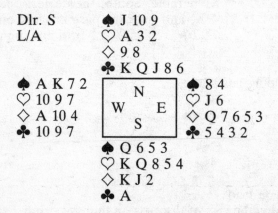

Dlr. S
L/A

♠ J 10 9
♡ A 3 2
◇ 9 8
♣ K Q J 8 6

♠ A K 7 2
♡ 10 9 7
◇ A 10 4
♣ 10 9 7

♠ 8 4
♡ J 6
◇ Q 7 6 5 3
♣ 5 4 3 2

♠ Q 6 5 3
♡ K Q 8 5 4
◇ K J 2
♣ A

Most defenders would probably put the contract one down by taking two spade tricks, a spade ruff and the

◇A also. However, if West can be certain of getting a diamond back straight away then the defence will do even better, for the play will take the following course: ♠ A-K, and the ♠7 ruffed, and a diamond returned to the ◇A. Now the ♠2 from West, forces North to ruff with the ♡A, so promoting a trump trick in the West hand.

♠ J 9 7	You are East, with both sides vulner-
♡ A 8 6	able. After a pass from you, South
◇ A 7 6 4 2	opens 1♠ and North responds 2◇.
♣ J 3	South jumps to 3♠ and North raises
	to 4♠.

The bidding:

South	North
1♠	2◇
3♠	4♠

West leads the ◇3 against South's contract of 4♠. You (East) win with the ◇A and South plays the ◇Q. Plan the defence.

Dlr. E   ♠ A 5
G/A   ♡ J 9
            ◇ K J 9 8 5
            ♣ K 6 5 4

                        ♠ J 9 7
                        ♡ A 8 6
                        ◇ A 7 6 4 2
                        ♣ J 3

Declarer has played as if he has a singleton diamond, but can this be true? Surely not; if declarer's ◇Q were a singleton then partner would have been dealt ◇ 10-3, in which case he would have led the ◇10. So it is partner who has the singleton and you can give him a ruff. The correct card to return is the ◇7, a suit preference signal to ensure that, when partner takes his ruff, he will return the higher ranking of the remaining suits (excluding trumps).

The full deal:

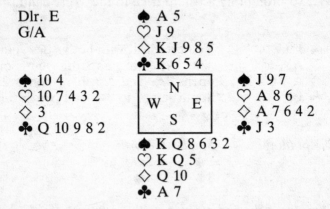

```
Dlr. E          ♠ A 5
G/A             ♡ J 9
                ◇ K J 9 8 5
                ♣ K 6 5 4
♠ 10 4                        ♠ J 9 7
♡ 10 7 4 3 2      N           ♡ A 8 6
◇ 3            W     E        ◇ A 7 6 4 2
♣ Q 10 9 8 2      S           ♣ J 3
                ♠ K Q 8 6 3 2
                ♡ K Q 5
                ◇ Q 10
                ♣ A 7
```

So the defence goes: ◇3 to the ◇A. ◇7 (signal) ruffed by West. ♡3 (4th highest) to the ♡A, and another diamond from East. If South ruffs low, he will be over-ruffed. If he ruffs high, the defenders will make a trump trick. What appears to be eleven solid tricks for North-South suddenly becomes only nine.

11 Defence Against Misfits Part 1 Partner has Bid a Suit

Considerations when defending against a misfit

There are some well-known misfit situations where the defence is clear. For example, if one defender has converted his partner's take-out double into a penalty double by passing:

West	North	East	South
1♡	Dbl	NB	NB

All the textbooks rightly say that North should lead a trump. Here, this is good advice, but there are many other difficult situations where there seems to be a paucity of advice, and many questions remain unanswered.

For example, should you *normally* lead a trump against a misfit, or is the case given above exceptional? Or does it depend on whether you are sitting over or under dummy's trumps or whether you think partner will be able to over-ruff dummy?

Or should you lead your long side suit? In any misfit situation, either you or your partner will have length in the opponent's trump suit and we have seen in an earlier situation (p. 118) how effective a forcing defence can be. Declarer is forced to trump and finishes up with fewer trumps than the defence, so losing control of the hand.

Fits and Misfits

Or should you try to snatch your side-suit tricks quickly against a misfit, before declarer takes discards on dummy's long suit?

Or, in contrast, should you lead dummy's long suit to use up declarer's entries in that suit and prevent him from taking discards after he has drawn trumps?

A study of hands from actual play will help to answer some of these questions. To do this, we will go back through some of the misfit hands that we have met earlier in the book and look at them in a fresh light, purely from the point of view of the defence, particularly the crucial opening lead. In this way we hope to produce some general principles that you can try out for yourself.

In this chapter we will consider the simpler types of situation where partner has bid a suit. Of course, you will often lead his suit, but we want to consider the reasons why you do so, and to identify the situations where it may pay you to look for something else.

♠ 2	On this hand (p. 116) your partner
♡ A 10 6	opened 1♠, the next player bid 2♡
◇ K 9 7 6	and you doubled for penalties. You
♣ K J 8 5 3	were advised to lead your partner's
	suit (your singleton spade).

Declarer won the first trick and led a trump, but you went straight up with your ace and put partner on lead twice in the minor suits, to give you two ruffs. Your two kings made tricks later.

The full deal:

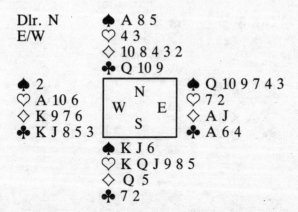

Dlr. N ♠ A 8 5
E/W ♡ 4 3
◇ 10 8 4 3 2
♣ Q 10 9

♠ 2   ♠ Q 10 9 7 4 3
♡ A 10 6   ♡ 7 2
◇ K 9 7 6   ◇ A J
♣ K J 8 5 3   ♣ A 6 4

♠ K J 6
♡ K Q J 9 8 5
◇ Q 5
♣ 7 2

On this hand your trumps are neither very long nor very strong and you have to use them for ruffing spades. The spade lead, therefore, is automatic.

♠ 8   When we met this hand earlier (p.
♡ 7 5   119) your partner opened 1♡ and the
◇ 9 7 6 5   next player chose 2♣. You didn't
♣ K J 9 8 6 5   have the general defensive strength
                   to double, so you passed, and 2♣
became the final contract. With all those trumps, you were not anxious to ruff and, if you had possessed a *safe* side-suit such as K-Q-J to lead from, you would have done so. However, any side-suit that you led might have helped declarer so you led your partner's suit (the ♡7) for the sake of safety, and this worked out all right in practice.

The full deal:

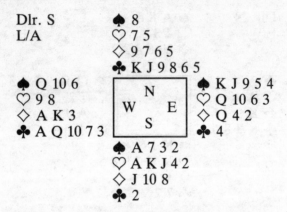

Dlr. S
L/A

North
♠ 8
♡ 7 5
♢ 9 7 6 5
♣ K J 9 8 6 5

West
♠ Q 10 6
♡ 9 8
♢ A K 3
♣ A Q 10 7 3

East
♠ K J 9 5 4
♡ Q 10 6 3
♢ Q 4 2
♣ 4

South
♠ A 7 3 2
♡ A K J 4 2
♢ J 10 8
♣ 2

As you can see, the lead of any side-suit would have given the same result on this particular hand. Nothing could prevent South from making his top tricks and North from making several trumps.

♠ 10	Partner opened 1♣ (p. 114) and
♡ Q 9 7 5	the next player chose 2♢, which
♢ A Q 9	you doubled. Again you selected
♣ K 10 7 5 2	partner's suit for the opening lead.

When we look at all four hands we can see that a club lead would have been just as good. The reason against it is, of course, that you didn't *know* partner had the ♣ A Q 8 when you chose, rightly, not to lead away from an unsupported honour.

The full deal:

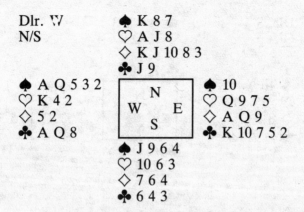

Dlr. W
N/S

♠ K 8 7
♡ A J 8
◇ K J 10 8 3
♣ J 9

♠ A Q 5 3 2
♡ K 4 2
◇ 5 2
♣ A Q 8

N
W   E
S

♠ 10
♡ Q 9 7 5
◇ A Q 9
♣ K 10 7 5 2

♠ J 9 6 4
♡ 10 6 3
◇ 7 6 4
♣ 6 4 3

However, if East had departed from the lead of his partner's suit, he might have chosen a heart instead of a club. That would have given declarer a trick, as often happens when a defender leads away from an unsupported honour. The point about leading partner's suit is that it is likely to be safe, and convenient, and it saves you from guessing. Although partner may well return his suit for you to ruff, he isn't forced to do so. If he thinks you have natural trump tricks, he is free to switch to something else.

A similar case arose on this hand from p. 84.

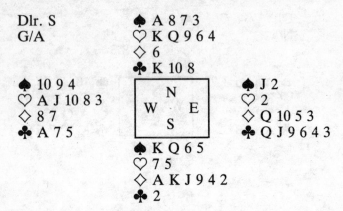

Dlr. S
G/A

♠ A 8 7 3
♡ K Q 9 6 4
◇ 6
♣ K 10 8

♠ 10 9 4
♡ A J 10 8 3
◇ 8 7
♣ A 7 5

N
W   E
S

♠ J 2
♡ 2
◇ Q 10 5 3
♣ Q J 9 6 4 3

♠ K Q 6 5
♡ 7 5
◇ A K J 9 4 2
♣ 2

South opened 1◇, West overcalled with 1♡ and North doubled. North led his partner's suit (the ◇6), South won with the ◇J but switched to his singleton ♣2, to try to obtain ruffs in his own, the shorter trump hand.

Postscript: Let's suppose that, instead of doubling 1♡, North had bid 1♠, and that North-South arrived at a spade contract. We said at the time (p. 85), without explaining it, that North-South would not be able to make 4♠ against accurate defence. We can now see how the defence would go. East leads the ♡2 to West's ♡A. West returns the ♡3 (a suit preference signal), so East ruffs and switches to a club. West wins and leads another heart. East ruffs with the ♠J, forcing South to over-ruff, and promoting a trump trick in the West hand.

On the hand shown opposite (from p. 102), South opened 1♠ and West bid 2♣, followed by two passes. South made a reopening double which was passed out. North led his partner's suit, the ♠9.

The full deal:

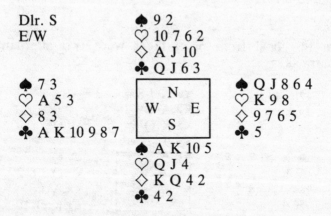

Dlr. S
E/W

North
♠ 9 2
♡ 10 7 6 2
♢ A J 10
♣ Q J 6 3

West
♠ 7 3
♡ A 5 3
♢ 8 3
♣ A K 10 9 8 7

East
♠ Q J 8 6 4
♡ K 9 8
♢ 9 7 6 5
♣ 5

South
♠ A K 10 5
♡ Q J 4
♢ K Q 4 2
♣ 4 2

Dummy's ♠J was played and South won with the ♠K. If he now mistakenly cashes the ♠A and leads another for his partner to ruff, this will have three bad effects, (a) West will discard a diamond loser, (b) North will give up one of his natural trump tricks, if he ruffs, and (c) dummy's ♠Q will be established and one of West's small hearts can be thrown on it later. So declarer will lose only five tricks (two spades, a spade ruff, one diamond and one club), and so make his doubled contract.

The correct defence is for South to switch suits at trick two. A diamond looks best, but it probably does not matter what he does provided he doesn't continue spades. The defence should now make two spade tricks, a heart trick, two diamonds and two clubs, and the contract is two down.

Many an unthinking defence, however, will go wrong on this hand with the 'automatic' spade lead, spade continuation and ruff. Appalling defence, you will think; it is obvious that North has simply made the apparently safe and convenient lead, and it's up to South to think about a switch. But so often one hears the unconvincing

alibi, 'Well, you led a spade, partner, so I thought you
wanted a ruff.'

On this deal from p. 89 there were two alternative
contracts.

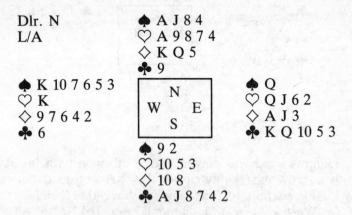

Dlr. N
L/A

North ♠ A J 8 4 ♡ A 9 8 7 4 ◇ K Q 5 ♣ 9

West ♠ K 10 7 6 5 3 ♡ K ◇ 9 7 6 4 2 ♣ 6

East ♠ Q ♡ Q J 6 2 ◇ A J 3 ♣ K Q 10 5 3

South ♠ 9 2 ♡ 10 5 3 ◇ 10 8 ♣ A J 8 7 4 2

North opened 1♡ and East overcalled with 2♣. South
and West passed, and North reopened with a take-out
double. East passed and South passed, to convert the
double into a penalty double.

If West passes (mistakenly) and South is on lead against
2♣, doubled, he will probably lead his partner's suit,
mainly for safety and convenience, as he is not too both-
ered about taking ruffs. When dummy's singleton ♡K
appears, North must put up his ace and switch immediately to a club to prevent a heart ruff in dummy.

If West rescues into 2♠ (probably also doubled) North
has no clear lead. The problem with leading a club (in a
sense, his partner's suit) is that although South will have
length in clubs, North doesn't know who has the top
clubs. If East has them, declarer may be able to get a
quick discard. So it's best for North to choose between
the red suits. The ◇K lead will work out well for the

defence. However, if North leads the ♡A instead and sees the ♡K fall from West, he must switch to a club before West can discard his club on dummy's ♡Q. A diamond trick and, hopefully, three trump tricks will roll in later for the defence.

On the hand shown below (see p. 121) South opened 1♡, West passed, North responded 1♠ and East intervened with 2♣. With no particular message to impart, South wisely decided to make use of the opponent's intervention by passing, allowing North to make the decision. North was glad of the opportunity to double 2♣.

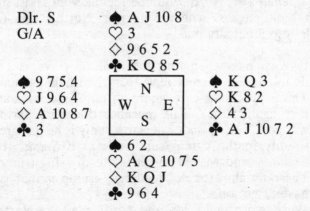

Dlr. S ♠ A J 10 8
G/A   ♡ 3
     ◇ 9 6 5 2
     ♣ K Q 8 5

♠ 9 7 5 4   ♠ K Q 3
♡ J 9 6 4 W N E ♡ K 8 2
◇ A 10 8 7   S ◇ 4 3
♣ 3   ♣ A J 10 7 2

     ♠ 6 2
     ♡ A Q 10 7 5
     ◇ K Q J
     ♣ 9 6 4

South has two attractive leads on this hand. He would be quite pleased to get a spade ruff in *his* hand, so the ♠6 lead, his partner's suit, is quite in order. Alternatively, the ◇K from the solid diamond sequence will work out just as well. East has only one entry into the dummy, and will finish up leading away from the high cards in his own hand. On either lead he will be lucky to make more than five or six tricks.

On the deal shown overleaf, and first described on p. 87, there were three possible contracts.

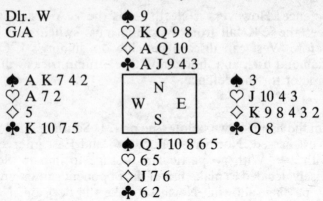

Dlr. W
G/A

```
                    ♠ 9
                    ♡ K Q 9 8
                    ◇ A Q 10
                    ♣ A J 9 4 3
♠ A K 7 4 2                          ♠ 3
♡ A 7 2              N               ♡ J 10 4 3
◇ 5             W         E          ◇ K 9 8 4 3 2
♣ K 10 7 5           S               ♣ Q 8
                    ♠ Q J 10 8 6 5
                    ♡ 6 5
                    ◇ J 7 6
                    ♣ 6 2
```

West opened 1♣, North doubled for take-out, East and South both passed, which converted North's take-out double into a penalty one.

(a) If West passes, so that the contract stays as 1♣, doubled, the correct lead from North is a trump. This is the classic case where a trump lead is mandatory against the misfit, because doubler's partner will pass, sitting under declarer, only if he has great solidity in the trump suit. It is as if *South* were declarer, and wished to set about drawing trumps. The only alibi for not leading a trump is that you haven't got one.

(b) West may run to 2♣ and North may double this (for penalties) and let's suppose that East and South pass. Against 2♣ doubled, the correct lead from North is ♣A and another. It's obvious from the bidding that East hates the spades and has a semi-fit for clubs. Otherwise he would have put his partner back to his first suit. So declarer will try to make extra tricks by leading spades from his hand and ruffing in dummy, and it's up to the defender on lead to stop this happening. In fact it is practically the only good rule in bridge that if an opponent gives

148

preference to his partner's second suit by passing, a trump lead will be the best defence.

(c) If East rescues his partner from 2♣ doubled, by bidding 2♦, South will be on lead and will have a less clear-cut choice. The lead of the unbid suit, hearts, is likely to be the choice that South will make.

Even so, East-West have found the best resting place; they have not reached too high a level and the weak hand is playing the contract in its own long trump suit, whilst his partner's high cards will still score.

Summary

When defending against a misfit, a high sequence, as against any other contract, will provide a good lead. If you are not lucky enough to have one, then partner's suit is usually safer than guessing which side suit to lead. The lead of partner's suit is acceptable even if the leader has trump length and does not particularly wish to ruff. He is not demanding the return of partner's suit; it is up to leader's partner to judge the situation.

When the defender who sits under declarer passes his partner's take-out double, a trump lead is mandatory. Similarly, when dummy has given preference to his partner's second suit by passing, a trump lead is best.

12 Defence Against Misfits
Part 2 Partner has not Bid a Suit

In this last chapter we continue the theme of defence against misfits. When we come to consider the possible outcomes of certain hands we shall find that, although they may be played in a misfitting contract, there may be other possible contracts on the same cards that are a semi-fit or even a good fit. We shall consider the defence to these too, as they occur, although the bulk of the discussion will concern misfits.

The choice of opening lead is made much more difficult if the lead is 'blind' that is, partner has not bid a suit and, in fact, no one can be right every time. There are also some hands where any lead will help declarer to some extent. However, in the majority of hands, the choice of opening lead is crucial to the defence, and it's essential to be on target as often as possible.

As we have seen before, you may be fortunate in having a high sequence from which to lead, in which case you can hardly go wrong, or responder may have given preference by passing, in which case you will be reaching for a trump. Unfortunately, you often have no such clear indications and you will be trying to choose between several unclear options.

We need to consider whether the defence against misfitting hands is a special case, or whether the same strategy should be used against both fits and misfits.

The first observation to be made about misfitting hands is that, by definition, dummy will be short of trumps, so the defenders can often look forward to some natural trump tricks. We have already seen that when defenders have long and solid trumps a trump lead is best (p. 148). Even if the defenders have rather gappy trumps, a trump lead seems not to cost a trick in the trump suit in a surprising number of cases. However it does put the ball in declarer's court, leaving the next move to him, and we have to question whether it is a good thing to give him this tempo. To answer this, one has to look at the whole hand.

Again, by definition, if the hand is a misfit, dummy will have a long suit facing a shortage in declarer's hand. If dummy has the tops in his suit, they will provide a rich source of discards. Thus the defence may need to make an effort to win their tricks in the other side suits before discards can be taken. They may therefore, need to be more attacking in lead style than is good for the nerves. We need to consider how much risk one should take to ensure that the side suit winners do not run away.

As in Chapter 11, we shall look back through some misfit hands that we have already met, and exmaine them from the defender's point of view, to see if we can draw any helpful conclusions.

We will begin with cases where there is a limited choice of leads because the opponents have bid three suits, and then move on to more problematical issues.

On the hand from p. 73 and shown overleaf, there was only one unbid suit:

Dlr. E
E/W

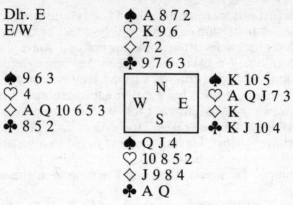

♠ A 8 7 2
♡ K 9 6
♢ 7 2
♣ 9 7 6 3

♠ 9 6 3
♡ 4
♢ A Q 10 6 5 3
♣ 8 5 2

♠ K 10 5
♡ A Q J 7 3
♢ K
♣ K J 10 4

♠ Q J 4
♡ 10 8 5 2
♢ J 9 8 4
♣ A Q

East opened 1♡ and West back-pedalled with a response of 1NT. East showed his second suit with a bid of 2♣ and West converted to 2♢, a command to pass. North has four choices of lead (1) dummy's first suit, (2) a trump, (3) the unbid suit (spades) or (4) dummy's second suit. Dummy's first suit is the most dangerous action as it will help to set it up; for instance if North leads the ♡6, dummy's ♡J will be played, the ♢K will be unblocked, followed by ♡A (on which West discards a spade) and then a heart ruff, to set up two winners in dummy. A trump lead also carries a risk, as it may trap an honour in partner's hand though, as the cards lie, that won't happen here. On balance, the leader will be choosing between options (3) and (4). The unbid suit is a reasonable choice on many hands but here North's holding in the suit is not appropriate. It's seldom wise to underlead an ace against a suit contract, so North would have to start with the ♠A if he decided to lead that suit. The most reasonable lead on this hand is dummy's second suit. East's clubs are likely to be shorter than his hearts, so the opportunity for discards is far less, and as can be seen on the hand shown above, a club will do no harm. North will lead the ♣9 or ♣7, depending on his lead style.

Similarly, on this hand from p. 71 there was again only one unbid suit.

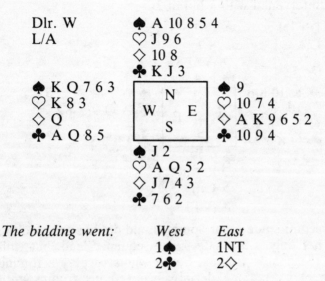

Dlr. W
L/A

♠ A 10 8 5 4
♡ J 9 6
◇ 10 8
♣ K J 3

♠ K Q 7 6 3
♡ K 8 3
◇ Q
♣ A Q 8 5

♠ 9
♡ 10 7 4
◇ A K 9 6 5 2
♣ 10 9 4

♠ J 2
♡ A Q 5 2
◇ J 7 4 3
♣ 7 6 2

The bidding went:

West	East
1♠	1NT
2♣	2◇

This contract is likely to make, but the defence should prevent overtricks. A spade lead would set up a winner in dummy, and should be avoided. A trump lead is safe, as the cards lie. The most likely lead from South is dummy's second suit, the ♣6 (middle-up down), and this will result in five tricks for the defence. South will avoid the lead of the unbid suit because he holds a tenace in it (and he has an alternative, reasonable lead in clubs).

Fits and Misfits

Moving on now to a different type of sequence, on the hand from p. 118 shown below, North opened 1NT and East intervened with a bid of 2♡:

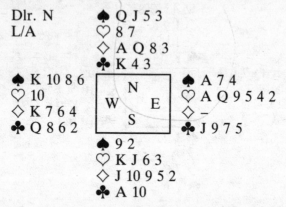

```
Dlr. N          ♠ Q J 5 3
L/A             ♡ 8 7
                ♢ A Q 8 3
                ♣ K 4 3
   ♠ K 10 8 6        N       ♠ A 7 4
   ♡ 10          W       E   ♡ A Q 9 5 4 2
   ♢ K 7 6 4         S       ♢ —
   ♣ Q 8 6 2                 ♣ J 9 7 5
                ♠ 9 2
                ♡ K J 6 3
                ♢ J 10 9 5 2
                ♣ A 10
```

We recommended that South should double and lead the ♢J; not only is it a safe top-of-sequence lead, but with four reasonable trumps, South wants to play a forcing defence, by making declarer shorten his trumps until South gains trump control.

We didn't consider other possible contracts, but if East-West play the popular 'Astro' convention, East will overcall with 2♣, to show hearts and a minor suit. West will respond 2NT (an artificial bid to enquire which minor) and East will bid 3♣. Now East-West will be playing in a fit, of course, and South's best lead will be the ♣A, on the grounds that the opponents have used a fit-finding convention (in this case, Astro) to find their best contract. Similarly, a trump lead is often useful against fits that have been reached via the unusual no-trump or other fit-finding manoeuvres, including the take-out double.

The ♣A, followed by ♣10 to North's ♣K and then a third round of clubs, is the best defence against the 3♣ contract because it cuts down heart ruffs in dummy and diamond ruffs in the East hand, leaving declarer to struggle with the remaining misfitting cards.

Defence Against Misfits

On the next hand from p. 92, there was a rescue:

Dlr. N
N/S

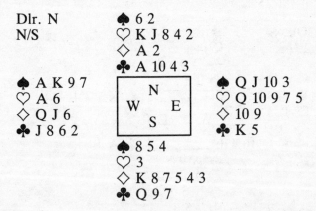

```
              ♠ 6 2
              ♡ K J 8 4 2
              ◇ A 2
              ♣ A 10 4 3
♠ A K 9 7                      ♠ Q J 10 3
♡ A 6          N              ♡ Q 10 9 7 5
◇ Q J 6      W   E            ◇ 10 9
♣ J 8 6 2      S              ♣ K 5
              ♠ 8 5 4
              ♡ 3
              ◇ K 8 7 5 4 3
              ♣ Q 9 7
```

North opened 1♡, East and South passed and West doubled for take-out. North passed but East also passed, to convert his partner's double into a penalty one, so South rescued into 2◇. The best defence is for West to lead the ♠A. When he sees that there are only two spades in dummy, he should switch immediately to the ◇Q, to prevent dummy from making a spade ruff.

If South had not rescued and the contract had been 1♡ doubled, East would probably have led the ♠Q, which is both safe, being top of a sequence, and also likely to be his partner's suit. He would have avoided a trump lead (up to declarer) or a short suit lead, as he would not wish to shorten his trumps by ruffing.

Fits and Misfits

There was also a rescue on the hand shown below, from p. 91.

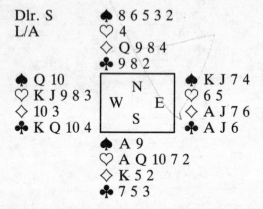

```
Dlr. S          ♠ 8 6 5 3 2
L/A             ♡ 4
                ♢ Q 9 8 4
                ♣ 9 8 2

♠ Q 10                        ♠ K J 7 4
♡ K J 9 8 3        N          ♡ 6 5
♢ 10 3         W     E        ♢ A J 7 6
♣ K Q 10 4         S          ♣ A J 6

                ♠ A 9
                ♡ A Q 10 7 2
                ♢ K 5 2
                ♣ 7 5 3
```

South opened 1♡, followed by two passes and a double from East. South passed, and West passed for penalties, so North rescued into 1♠, doubled by East.

East is likely to avoid the lead of a trump up to declarer, although it would do no harm as the cards lie. Similarly, a heart lead *might* have cost a trick if South had ♡ A-K, as North would quickly have discarded a club. On the face of it, the choice is between one of the two side suits, diamonds or clubs. It is unwise to under-lead an ace against a suit contract, but East can play an ace to see which suit is best. If he happens to choose the ♣A, West will encourage. If he chooses the ♢A, West will realise it is to take a look, as the ♢K is in dummy, so he will discourage, and East will switch to a club.

Postscript: It is often rightly stated that the purpose in life of an ace is to kill a king, so the lead of an ace, 'beating the air', is not to be undertaken lightly. Thus, if East chooses the ♢A, North-South will now make both the ♢K and the ♢Q. However, a trump or a heart lead might equally have cost a trick, so again it is a matter of balancing the risks.

If the rescue had come the other way about, as on the hand from p. 82, the leader has a difficult choice.

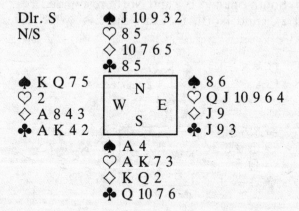

Dlr. S
N/S

♠ J 10 9 3 2
♡ 8 5
♢ 10 7 6 5
♣ 8 5

♠ K Q 7 5
♡ 2
♢ A 8 4 3
♣ A K 4 2

♠ 8 6
♡ Q J 10 9 6 4
♢ J 9
♣ J 9 3

♠ A 4
♡ A K 7 3
♢ K Q 2
♣ Q 10 7 6

South opened 1♡, doubled for take-out by West and passed for penalties by East. South made an SOS redouble and North rescued to 1♠.

If this becomes the final contract and East has to lead, he may well wish to try a side suit. However, with no ace to lead to take a look, he really is on a guess and if he gets it wrong there is no way of correcting it. For this reason he is likely to fall back on the safe, top-of-sequence lead of the ♡Q instead, which does no harm, as the cards lie.

Postscript: No lead is likely to defeat 1♠, so North-South have found themselves a good spot.

Fits and Misfits

Continuing with hands where there are at least two unbid suits from which to choose, there is this problem from p. 65, South opened 1◇ and North responded 1♠. South rebid 2◇ and North foolishly bid 2♠, which everyone passed.

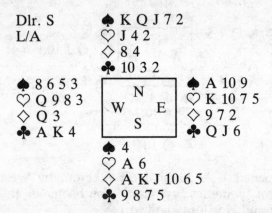

```
Dlr. S          ♠ K Q J 7 2
L/A             ♡ J 4 2
                ◇ 8 4
                ♣ 10 3 2
♠ 8 6 5 3                      ♠ A 10 9
♡ Q 9 8 3         N            ♡ K 10 7 5
◇ Q 3          W     E         ◇ 9 7 2
♣ A K 4           S            ♣ Q J 6
                ♠ 4
                ♡ A 6
                ◇ A K J 10 6 5
                ♣ 9 8 7 5
```

This is an easy hand for the defence. East simply avoids leading up to North's trumps (although again it would not have cost a trick) and avoided dummy's long suit. The ♣Q looks natural, and having made three clubs, the defenders should switch to a heart.

158

Only two suits were mentioned also on this hand from
p. 69:

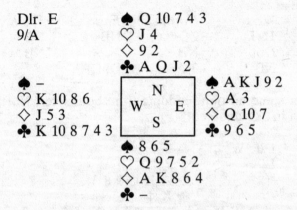

Dlr. E
9/A

North: ♠ Q 10 7 4 3 ♡ J 4 ◇ 9 2 ♣ A Q J 2

West: ♠ — ♡ K 10 8 6 ◇ J 5 3 ♣ K 10 8 7 4 3

East: ♠ A K J 9 2 ♡ A 3 ◇ Q 10 7 ♣ 9 6 5

South: ♠ 8 6 5 ♡ Q 9 7 5 2 ◇ A K 8 6 4 ♣ —

East opened 1♠ and West dredged up a 1NT response.
East unwisely bid 2♠ and West signed off in 3♣. When
we discussed this hand earlier, we said that North had a
difficult lead, and would have to guess between the two
unbid suits. A heart would give declarer the contract, as
he would discard his two losing diamonds on dummy's
spades, whereas a diamond would defeat declarer straight
away. However, as we have seen already in this chapter,
North could have deferred his decision. If he is prepared
to play his ♣A at trick 1, he will quickly see that a switch
to diamonds is the only hope.

One would normally never lead from a trump holding
such as A-Q-J-2, so why should North break the rules on
this hand? The answer is that the bidding indicates that
West is likely to have six clubs, so North will probably
make three club tricks whether or not he leads the ace.
It is true that there is a slight risk that North may kill a
singleton club honour in the South hand but this has to
be weighed against the risk of choosing the wrong red
suit with a 'blind' lead.

Fits and Misfits

On the hand shown below (from p. 94) West opened 1NT and, the bidding took an unusual course.

West	North	East	South
1NT	2◇	NB	NB
Dbl	NB	2♡	NB
NB	3◇	Dbl	

After some unsound bidding from both sides, North finished in 3◇ doubled.

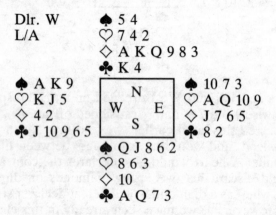

```
Dlr. W          ♠ 5 4
L/A             ♡ 7 4 2
                ◇ A K Q 9 8 3
                ♣ K 4
♠ A K 9                         ♠ 10 7 3
♡ K J 5            N            ♡ A Q 10 9
◇ 4 2         W       E         ◇ J 7 6 5
♣ J 10 9 6 5      S            ♣ 8 2
                ♠ Q J 8 6 2
                ♡ 8 6 3
                ◇ 10
                ♣ A Q 7 3
```

East didn't want to lead a trump but had the choice of three other suits. A club would have been bad for the defence, as declarer would have cashed ♣K, ♣A and ♣Q, and discarded a major suit loser from his own hand. However, the implication from the bidding was that West had an interest in the major suits, so East tried the ♠3. The defence cashed their top tricks in hearts and spades, and picked up a trump trick later.

It's interesting to consider the alternative contract. As we said on p. 94, South missed the opportunity to double East's contract of 2♡. You may think South has an automatic lead now, the ◇10, his partner's suit, but this is not so. If East can engineer two diamond ruffs in dummy,

he will make his eight tricks. South's correct lead against
2♡ by East is a trump. The opponents have used a fit-
finding convention, West's take-out double, to reach their
contract, and a trump lead is the best defence.

Finally, another hand with a wide variety of choices is
this deal from p. 120.

East opened 1NT and this was passed round to North,
who made a penalty double. East and South passed, and
West bid 2♣. North wisely decided to pass this around
to his partner, who doubled.

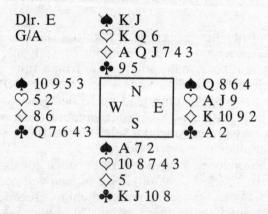

```
Dlr. E        ♠ K J
G/A           ♡ K Q 6
              ♢ A Q J 7 4 3
              ♣ 9 5
♠ 10 9 5 3         N        ♠ Q 8 6 4
♡ 5 2       W         E     ♡ A J 9
♢ 8 6             S        ♢ K 10 9 2
♣ Q 7 6 4 3                ♣ A 2
              ♠ A 7 2
              ♡ 10 8 7 4 3
              ♢ 5
              ♣ K J 10 8
```

For the lead, North avoided a trump up to declarer or a
diamond away from his tenace and so had to choose
between the unbid side suits, hearts or spades. He chose
the ♡K and this was good enough to give the defence
six tricks. It is hardly likely that anyone would find a
spade lead from ♠ K-J but it is interesting to conjecture
that if North had played the ♢A to see dummy, he might
then have realised the necessity to switch to the ♠K and
snatch a spade ruff.

Conclusions

You will recognise misfits, even if partner has not bid, because the opponents will be bidding your long suit(s), or bidding at cross purposes with each other, as in many of the hands in this chapter. You will also know there is a misfit if a take-out double has been passed for penalties.

If you are on lead and have a high sequence you should often choose to lead it, on grounds of safety. Against any contract, it is often the only lead that is both safe and yet, at the same time, attacking. Against misfits, however, there are a number of other factors to bear in mind:

(a) If partner has passed your take-out double, sitting under declarer, lead a trump. He will only have passed if he is really solid in the trump suit.

(b) Even if the bidding goes 1 of a suit-NB-NB-Dbl, NB-NB-NB, a trump lead up to declarer seems to do little harm in a surprising number of cases, but you may prefer to lead a side suit (partner has 'bid' them all).

(c) If the opponents have bid three suits, for example 1♡-1NT, 2♣-2♢, your choice of lead will normally lie between the unbid suit or dummy's second suit. Your holding in these suits will determine your selection.

(d) If the opponents have bid two suits, for example 1♢-1♠, 2♢-2♠, it is unwise to lead dummy's long suit because of the danger of discards, and you will normally try an unbid suit. Your chances of getting the defence right will be improved if you have an ace that you can play to get a look at dummy and to see if partner encourages. He, for his part, should realise your lead is speculative, and not necessarily expect you to have the king too. The situation is rather similar to that in which the opponents have opened with a gambling 3NT, and you are not sure in which suit to attack.

(e) Remember (from Chapter 11) that if opponents have given preference by passing, you should almost always lead a trump. Dummy has a semi-fit for declarer's second suit and a misfit for his first suit.

You will not *always* make the right lead by following the guidelines given here, but, in analysing these hands, our aim has been to help you to avoid the illogical leads and to steer you towards a limited number of choices that are likely to be most profitable for the defence.

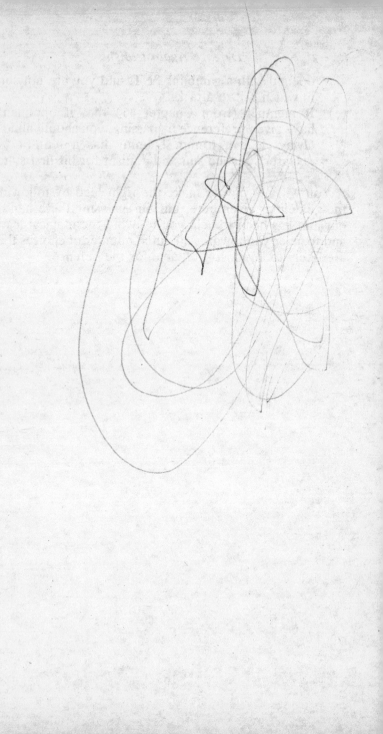